THE TERRARIUM BOOK

The. Terrarium Book

Charles M. Evans
with Roberta Lee Pliner

Illustrations by Betty Fraser

RANDOM HOUSE
New York

Terrariums on the cover designed by
Roland Bouchard, Charles M. Evans
and Anthony Mazzariello.

Library of Congress Cataloging in Publication Data

Evans, Charles M.
The terrarium book.
1. Glass gardens. I. Pliner, Roberta Lee, joint
author. II. Title.
SB417.E9   635.9'85   72-11388
ISBN 0-394-48564-2 (hardbound)
ISBN 0-394-70968-3 (paperbound)

Manufactured in the United States of America
Design by Bernard Klein
4 5 6 7 8 9

For Doris Prince

Contents

THE TERRARIUM BOOK

A nineteenth-century Wardian Case

1/
The Terrarium

A terrarium is one living plant growing and thriving inside a sealed glass container. A terrarium is also a landscape under glass—a woodland, a desert, a tropical jungle, or a gardener's fantasy.

Terrarium containers can be antique junk-shop finds or chemist's flasks, Steuben crystal or old aquarium tanks. Whatever their original purpose, if within their walls there is a garden growing, they become terrariums: glass containers encompassing complete miniature environments.

The terrarium we know today is directly descended from the Wardian case developed in the nineteenth century. But, even earlier than that, around 500 B.C., terrariums had appeared in Greece, at the annual festival of Adonis. Statues of Aphrodite's slain lover were decorated for the festival with small plants cultivated under glass bell-shaped jars. These small glass gardens were tended for eight days, then neglected until they withered. Eventually, they were thrown into the Aegean Sea as a symbol of the death and regeneration of all vegetative life.

If the Greeks had looked after their small terrariums longer, the world might have realized the horticultural

the history of terrariums

The Terrarium

3

possibilities of terrariums somewhat earlier than the nineteenth century, when Dr. Nathaniel Ward, a London surgeon whose avocation was natural history, accidentally made the discovery. One day in 1829 Dr. Ward decided that he wanted to see an adult sphinx moth hatch from a chrysalis. Accordingly, he buried the cocoon in damp soil in a glass jar, which he covered with a metal top. Out of the soil sprouted some grass and a fern, and the doctor promptly lost interest in the moth. For the next four years the grass and fern prospered with no additional water and no influx of fresh air until, during Dr. Ward's absence from home, the metal top rusted, thereby allowing rain to come in and ultimately rot the plants. By that time Dr. Ward was fascinated with the possibilities of cultivating certain ferns and other plants considered impossible to grow in the polluted sooty air of nineteenth-century London. He continued to experiment successfully with over a hundred different fern species.

In 1832 he tried shipping plants in glass containers. Filling two large glass cases with ferns and grasses, he sent them to Sydney, Australia, by way of the Cape of Good Hope—at that time an eight-month sea journey. The cases were lashed to the deck throughout the voyage; though they had to weather rather severe changes in temperature, the plants remained intact and thriving. Australian colleagues returned the cases to Dr. Ward, reversing the route under similar conditions and with equal success.

In 1842 Dr. Ward published his results, and his small portable greenhouses came to be known as Wardian cases. By the middle of the century the Wardian cases were being shipped all over the world. In particular, the Indian tea growers, who had never been able to ship their plants successfully, now found themselves a world-wide industry. Similarly, Chinese banana trees found their way into the Fijian and Samoan islands, and Brazilian rubber trees were introduced into Ceylon. Meanwhile, ornamental plant growers in Europe and America profited enormously from the successful intercontinental exchange of local plant specimens.

As a result of Dr. Ward's efforts, the contemporary indoor gardener anywhere in the world has a wide choice of plants to grow indoors and an excellent method of maintaining many very delicate specimens that refuse to adapt to the hot, dry atmosphere of modern central heating and air-conditioning systems. The closed glass container conserves moisture and humidity, shields plants from drafts and abrupt temperature changes, and still admits light. It provides a completely protected environment for any plant small enough to fit within it.

Now, it happens that some plants do not need quite that much protection, yet you may be fascinated with the idea of creating a small window-sill landscape with such plants. As you will see, you can make all sorts of adjustments in planting and maintaining a terrarium in order to accommodate lots of different plants. Those that need constantly and evenly damp soil but less humidity will thrive nicely in a partly open terrarium. Some that need relatively little moisture and humidity can be grown in a very open terrarium.

What is really exciting about terrariums is all the different things you can do with them. There is a treasure of beautiful possibilities. Consider, for example, the elegance of a single perfect miniature rose blooming under a crystal bell jar. Or a fascinating tangle of lichens, mosses, wild violets and hepatica in a terrarium case of your own design and construction. Perhaps you might appreciate the spectacle of a carnivorous pitcher plant embedded in its own little glass-enclosed bog trapping your live flies and mosquitoes or even hamburger meat.

Once you have mastered the art of putting together a simple small terrarium, you can take off with odd-shaped containers and special decorative schemes, such as evergreen seedlings and partridgeberry for Christmas or small begonias and lilies for Easter. You can have terrariums in bloom using African violets, Mexican foxgloves, or Spathe flower. Or for temporary color, you can add cut flowers with shortened stems to a green terrarium where they will last much longer than in a vase.

The Terrarium

**what are
terrariums
good for?**

Not only are terrariums lovely; they have interesting prac- tical aspects. First is the comforting thought of having some house plants that are relatively or even totally ne- glectable. Terrarium plants will delight the apartment dweller who has no control of his heating levels and who has trouble keeping even the easiest-to-grow plants alive, much less growing.

Then there are the possibilities of children's projects. Children can learn a lot about both indoor and outdoor gardening from planting and taking care of a miniature garden in a glass case. For years schools have been giving children cut-down milk cartons in which to start seeds. How much prettier—and instructive—it would be to use inexpensive plastic drinking glasses so that the children could see the root systems as well as the plant tops develop.

If you like health foods, a terrarium is a marvelous environment for growing bean or lentil sprouts. Use damp blotting paper as the planting medium and keep the closed container in a warm, dimly lit location until seeds sprout.

Small closed terrariums that take up little room and require little or no maintenance make perfect sickroom gifts, or, for the convalescent, you can make up a terrarium kit that encompasses plants, container, tools and soil components. Even a bedridden patient could manage a terrarium small enough that its parts could be handled on a bed-tray.

**vivariums:
terrariums
with animals**

Everyone wants to know whether you can include small animals in a terrarium. One might say, with certain res- ervations, that it's possible. Adding small animals, such as baby turtles or chameleons, to the terrarium gives an added dimension to the mini-environment. The vivarium is the dry-land equivalent of an aquarium. Perhaps, if you have had no luck with your tropical fish, you might even consider converting your fish tank into a terrarium or vivarium.

The Terrarium Book

Animals that can be managed in a vivarium include horned toads and geckos, which will live compatibly with desert plants; chameleons, salamanders and turtles, which will be happy wandering among tropical foliage plants; and tree frogs (if you can catch them), newts and woods toads, which will complement woodland plantings.

Turtles need small ponds; chameleons, something to climb on; salamanders, something to crawl under. Toads and lizards want some clean dry sand with a few pebbles to rest upon; both of these as well as frogs want plenty of room and places to hide when they're hibernating. Newts particularly like bog gardens; you might try them with a carnivorous planting for a really exotic atmosphere.

Whatever you choose, there is one all-important consideration you must take into account before purchasing even one animal: they all need *live* food. In summer or if you live in a more or less tropical climate, this may not be a serious problem if you're willing to catch flies and other flying insects for your vivarium pets.

But in temperate zones, without a supply of live food, these pets will certainly do great damage to your planting —or else they'll die. Also, unless the planting is rather well spaced out and the plants very sturdy, several animals confined even in a large terrarium may damage plants simply by trampling them.

Ecologically, life in a vivarium is not fair to the animals. Most ordinary home conditions cannot provide the animals with the environment that enables them to live longer, happier lives if left to their own devices in their native habitats (notwithstanding stories about turtles who have survived even the trauma of being flushed down a toilet). Think twice and hard before setting up a vivarium, unless you're trying to concoct a witches' brew or you really can provide the most optimal conditions and are willing to replace damaged plants.

You can use a terrarium as a nursery, a small greenhouse that provides a controlled environment for starting cuttings and bulbs and raising small, tender seedlings. The terrarium-cum-nursery should ideally be a square or rectangular glass case, such as a fish tank, that can be located in a well-lit window or provided with its own fluorescent-light unit. If the case is large enough, the nursery can also serve as a hospital for ailing potted plants, which must be isolated from healthy ones while being treated or which need a more protected environment than they normally require.

Terrariums can be fun. When you begin making them, you might find yourself launched on an absorbing and rewarding new project, one that will increase the scope of your indoor gardening. Someday you may use terrariums in ways no one else has ever thought of.

Drosera filiformis

Ficus diversifolia

Begonia boweri

2/
Containers

Starting a terrarium poses a question somewhat akin to that of the chicken and the egg. Does the container define the plants or do the plants define the container? It's always easier to start with the container. The choice of plants may be limited by environmental factors, but the choice of a container is mainly a matter of space and preference. Many kinds of containers are available; essentially any clear glass container that can be readily opened and closed will serve for a terrarium. A crystal brandy snifter from Tiffany's makes a much more elegant bottle garden than a jam jar—but there are jam jars and jam jars. You might have a very nice one that will house miniature ferns or blooming sinningias in great style.

The most important limitation is color. Clear glass transmits all available light, and without light no plant will survive. Colored containers, even those in very muted colors, reduce light intensity and tend to transmit their own colors while absorbing all other colors. Red glass would transmit red, and light at the red end of the color spectrum produces unnaturally elongated, leggy plants, which you do not want in a terrarium.

If your heart is set on constructing a terrarium in a colored glass container, at least use one of a very muted color and restrict your planting to low-light plants. Bear in mind that if you use dark-colored glass, you won't be able to see the plants anyway. Do you remember, for example, the first time you poured dry sherry out of a dark bottle and were surprised to discover the sherry was a light amber color?

Wine bottles often appeal to terrarium gardeners. A wine bottle can be a beautiful terrarium if the glass is clear or muted. If it is green, as so many are, it will transmit green light that plants can make no use of. The green glass will block out red and blue light without which no plant can survive.

The one alternative to clear glass is Plexiglass or Lucite. It scratches easily, so you must be careful in handling and cleaning. For cleaning, soft, clean, lint-free cloths, such as chamois or old diapers, work very well. Plexiglass units designed for terrariums are just beginning to appear on the market; presumably the selection will be greater in due time. Meanwhile, you can make your own by getting suppliers to cut pieces to fit your design.

Perhaps you already have plants for a terrarium, or at least you already know which plants you want to start with in your terrarium. Then the chicken-and-egg process is reversed; your choice of container must be of such a size and shape that it conforms to the general dimensions of the plant. Keep in mind also that plants will grow; a tall plant that looks like a seedling this week may be shoving up the cover of a low terrarium next month.

As long as the size of a tank-type case is appropriate, any terrarium plant will do well in one. The large fish tanks give you the greatest scope, because their breadth and height will permit you to grow colorful caladiums and anthuriums and some of the taller ferns or dracaenas, as well as low-growing, bushy plants and ground covers for variety. Small cases will house miniature begonias, small ferns and creeping selaginella. Some of the really tiny woodlands specimens will do beautifully in a small terrarium case—one that can be permanently closed for minimal care.

The simplest terrarium to establish and plant is a large rectangular case. The easiest to obtain are aquarium tanks; you might even have an old, slightly leaky one that with a little resealing with commercial aquarium sealant would make an excellent terrarium. If you buy a tank, look for tall, skinny shapes; somehow they seem to make better-looking terrariums and they are more likely to fit on window sills. Store-bought tanks can be purchased at any price; the very elaborate (and expensive) ones are equipped with artificial lighting and humidifying units. If space is a problem in your home, try constructing your own terrarium case from glass or Plexiglass. Plexiglass is particularly easy to work with and you can have the pieces cut to fit.

tanks and cases

For a Victorian effect, harking back to the old Wardian cases, you might search antique stores for old curio cabinets. These are usually oak-, nickel- or mahogany-framed cabinets that can be found in floor, wall-hung or table models in a wide variety of designs. All have glass fronts and sides and hinged doors that are wide enough to insert and remove any object that will fit in the case. Originally designed to display jewelry, china collections or small antique bibelots, they make really distinctive terrariums, especially if you have very good light. An epoxy sealant can be used to seal the planting area to make it water tight, or a galvanized metal pan can be constructed to fit the inside bottom of the case.

Moisture in open tank-type cases evaporates much more quickly than in other types of containers. If you're working with cacti and succulents, this might be an advantage, but with most other plants it becomes especially important to provide a well-fitted cover. If your tank

Containers

13

does not come with its own cover, a glazier can cut one to fit, quite inexpensively. You can make a temporary cover from plastic food wrap in case you forgot about the cover before planting or if it's Sunday and the glazier's is closed.

bowls, round shapes

A glass bowl whose opening is large enough for you to get your hand in is as easy to plant as a rectangular case. Besides, bowls and other round containers are interesting shapes to work with, and because they have smaller openings than tank cases do, they can be left open with less humidity loss. Glass globes and oversized brandy snifters are traditional round-shaped terrariums. But depending on the dimensions of your plants, there are many other possibilities. Wide-mouthed juice pitchers, crystal beer mugs, certain flower vases—once you're interested, you

will start seeing terrarium possibilities in every glass container you encounter. You might also check scientific laboratory equipment suppliers; they stock some containers that would lend themselves very nicely to growing plants.

As with tank containers, the wider the opening, the more moisture the bowl container will lose. As the point of the terrarium is to conserve moisture, you should provide a cover, which again a glazier can cut to fit.

Bowl terrariums seem to call for low-growing leafy plants, such as African violets or shrubby, woody types, such as mistletoe, fig or coral berry. In a small oval or globular container, one of these plants might be nicely displayed if surrounded by a mossy ground cover and some pretty pebbles.

A variation on a bowl terrarium is a dome terrarium. The bowl, inverted, becomes a cover for plants set into a tray, saucer or anything deep enough to accommodate soil and root systems. Set your plants into the saucer just as you would into a flower pot; however, to conserve moisture the saucer should be nonporous. For the dome, you might use cake-dish and cheese-dish covers, or you can also buy, in garden and department stores, ready-made dome units in tall, skinny shapes that adapt beautifully to tall plants that are difficult to fit into the more conventional squat terrariums.

One type of dome terrarium on the market is a small plastic greenhouse. The bottom is a green plastic tray, and the top, which lifts off, is clear plastic, shaped like a tiny greenhouse. These can be purchased separately or in kits equipped with seeds, cactus cuttings and tiny pots. Children's stores sell them for educational projects. The design isn't exactly elegant, but these are easy to work with for practice or for a nursery terrarium.

bottles

Bottles and jars make interesting terrariums, but they are also among the most difficult to plant and maintain.

Containers

Save them for the time when you feel you have mastered the principles of terrarium planting in simple square containers.

Bottle terrariums are often called bottle gardens and they require some of the same tools and techniques that are used in building ship models in bottles. If the very thought of constructing a model ship in a wine bottle makes you tremble, confine your terrarium projects to bowls, pitchers or tanks. If you must use a bottle, try to find a wide-necked one. If your hand fits in, so much the better; in any case, the wider the mouth, the easier it is to poke tools in.

The shape of the bottle should match that of the plant because it is difficult to prune or cut back rampantly growing plants in bottles. Anticipate the plant's future size and plan your bottle garden accordingly. If the bottle has a relatively wide neck, pruning is easier, and, in that case, podocarpus and other plants that lend themselves to pruning or dwarf plants (such as sinningia) make good bottle-garden subjects.

Bottles can be, of course, as modest as that old jam jar, as elaborate as a crystal decanter. They needn't even have flat bottoms; round-heel shapes make nice hanging displays. Hardware for hanging should accommodate the fairly considerable weight of a fully planted, newly watered garden—soil and water are heavy.

Even the homely screw-cap jar can be used. Cut the top off with one of those inexpensive bottle-cutting tools you will find at hardware, houseware or department stores. Then cut a new glass cover to fit the new, nicer-shaped jar.

Very narrow-necked bottles may be left open; they will lose very little moisture. If they seem to dry out too quickly, they can be corked. Corks come in all sizes.

Or, if you're hanging a screw-cap bottle just as it is, you can camouflage the screw grooves with hemp rope, leather thongs or copper wire. Wind the rope around the grooves, which then serve to hold the rope in place. Extend the ends of the rope to the length you need for hanging the bottle.

The Terrarium Book

Some quite nice antique bottles may be badly stained. Do not reject them on that account. If ordinary cleaning methods do not help, try solutions of Clorox, toilet-bowl cleaners, rust removers, or Dip-it (a product sold for cleaning coffeepots).

In addition to cleaning, it is important to check new as well as old containers for leakage. Fill the container with water and let it stand for an hour or so. Note where the water leaks out, if at all, and use aquarium sealant to patch those spots.

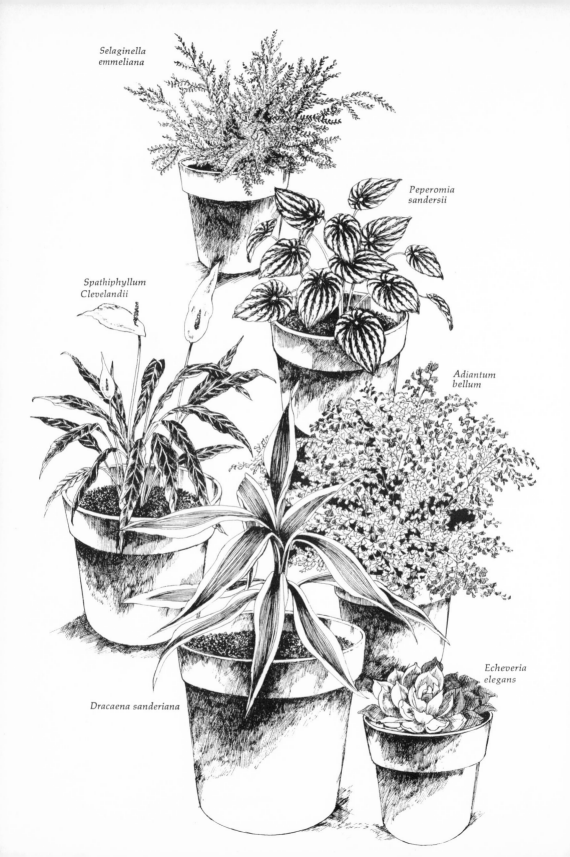

Selaginella emmeliana

Peperomia sandersii

Spathiphyllum Clevelandii

Adiantum bellum

Dracaena sanderiana

Echeveria elegans

3/
Plants

Some terrarium plants are sun babies, growing tall and stretching their sturdy leaves toward any bright light. Some prefer to nestle in the shade of larger plants, perhaps peeking at the sun for just a few hours early in the morning. Others creep along the ground, winding their way hither and yon, sometimes twining their delicate leaves around the trunks of tall plants, sometimes climbing up and covering terrarium walls.

Several plants will live and grow for years in a tightly sealed terrarium that requires no attention; you will enjoy watching them progress from dormant, quiet seasons to active, growing seasons. Other plants, especially desert cacti and many succulents, want fairly dry conditions. Terrariums with such plants should be open; this gives you the chance not only to look at your plants but to sniff them, for cacti and succulents in the right growing conditions often send up sweetly scented flowers.

Many plants may be collected from local bogs and woods; small specimens will thrive in terrariums and grow nicely, though not as rampantly as indoor plants. Some plants are meat-eaters, and some have so many colors that they look like Joseph's coat.

For most of you, there will be many choices of terrarium gardens. The major critical limitation on your
choice of plants is that all the plants in any one container
must thrive in the same cultural conditions, that is, their
soil, temperature, light and humidity requirements must
be the same.

In the following pages, plants are ·assembled accord-
ing to their similar cultural needs. Would you like a terrarium on a cool, sunny porch? Then examine the plant
lists that call for high light and cool temperatures. Is your
apartment overheated, and do your windows face north?
Look at the lists for low-light and warm-temperature
plants.

All plants described in this book are readily available
from house-plant stores, garden centers, or mail-order catalogs advertised in garden and shelter magazines. Woodlands plants are, of course, specific to wherever you live;
you may find some interesting terrarium specimens in your
locality that are not mentioned in this book. Don't be
afraid to try them. Common names of plants, wherever
they exist, are mentioned and listed in the Appendix but
it's really better to use scientific Latin names (spell them
if you can't pronounce them) when purchasing or order-
ing plants. As a good gardener of terrariums or otherwise,
it would serve you well to learn to use scientific names.
When searching for a particular plant, either in local shops
or through mail-order catalogs, the one plant designation
everyone in the trade recognizes and refers to is the scientific name. You might ask for a miniature African violet
and receive a plant that requires the roominess of a fish-
tank terrarium, but if you request a *Sinningia pusilla*,
you will get a tiny bloomer perfect for a covered crystal
compote dish.

light   Light is the first thing you must consider before choosing
plants. The kind of light the terrarium needs depends on

the plants, but conversely, the plants that you choose will depend on the light you can provide for the terrarium. In general, plants can be sorted into low-light, medium-light and high-light groups.

Natural light is outdoor light that the terrarium receives through windows. If it is daylight with no direct sun, it is probably low light. If there is sun in the windows for part of the day, the light is considered medium, but if the sun shines in for most or all of the day, the light is high.

Most terrarium plants fall into the medium-light group. That designation will also suit plants we have called low-light plants, though these will also adjust to and survive lower light intensities; in medium light, they simply grow more sturdily and quickly. The point is that you can, to some extent, mix plants in different categories, providing your light source is adequate for the plants needing the higher light intensity.

Use common sense if you move plants to higher light than they've been accustomed to. Ordinarily, you should expose plants to increased light intensities very gradually. When you understand how much light is required by a specific plant, you may, with due caution, place it in a higher light situation, but do not move it from a low to a high intensity light or move it too quickly. This is particularly true if you want to grow medium-light plants in a high-light situation. Although it's no great trick to accustom low-light plants to medium light, it's extremely difficult to persuade most medium-light plants to behave in high light. The increase must take place on a very careful, experimental basis.

If your natural-light source is insufficient for the terrarium plants you wish to grow, consider using artificial light. You may already have an artificial-light setup that would do well for terrarium plantings; if not, light arrangements for terrariums can be easily set up.

Low-light plants are those that will survive in the light usually received from north windows or in the interior of a room with sunny windows. A good indication that you have low light is that it is a good reading light without electric lamps. Few plants can survive with only low light. A little supplementary light is necessary to ensure actual growth. Plants that can be used in a low-light situation include:

Aglaonema	Marchantia	Scindapsus
Chamaedorea	Philodendron	Spathiphyllum
Dracaena	Pittosporum	Syngonium
Euonymus	Sansevieria	

Chamaedorea elegans 'bella'

Aglaonema 'Fransher'

Euonymus japonicus medio-pictus

Pittosporum tobira

Philodendron oxycardium

Medium-light plants are those that grow in sun for a few hours a day, such as morning sun from an east window, and strong daylight the remainder of the day. Many plants in the group listed below can slowly be adjusted to lower or higher light.

Acorus	Fittonia	Pellaea
Adiantum	Gaultheria	Pellionia
Ajuga	Goodyera	Peperomia
Allophytum	Hedera	Pilea
Anthurium	Helxine	Pistia
Aphelandra	Hydrocleys	Podocarpus
Ardisia	Hydrocotyle	Polypodium
Arisaema	Lemna	Pteris
Azolla	Maranta	Salvinia
Begonia	Marsilea	Saintpaulia
Buxus	Mimosa	Sarracenia
Caladium	Mitchella	Saxifraga
Calathea	Myriophyllum	Scilla
Ceropegia	Myrsine	Selaginella
Chlorophytum	Myrtus	Serissa
Cryptanthus	Nasturtium	Sinningia
Darlingtonia	Nepenthes	Stenotaphrum
Dichorisandra	Nertera	Streptocarpus
Drosera	Ophiopogon	Tradescantia
Episcia	Osmanthus	Zebrina
Ficus		

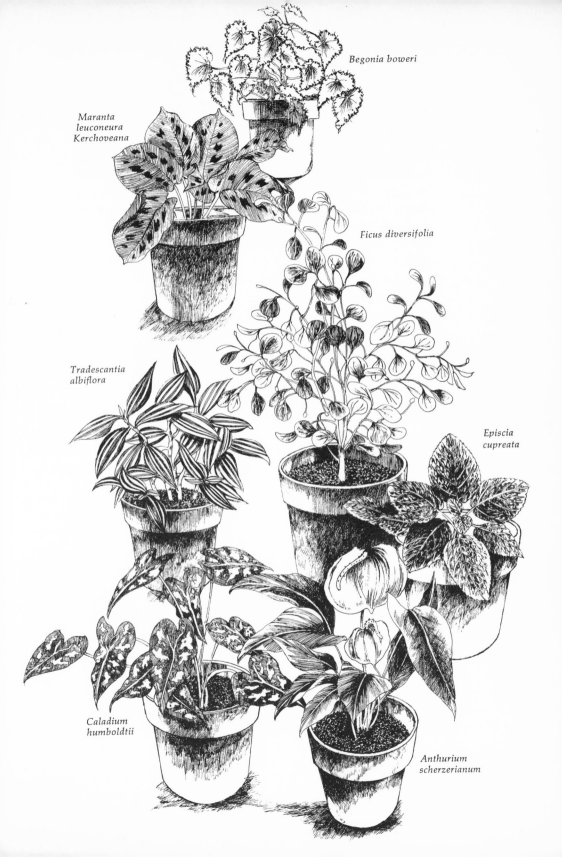

Begonia boweri

Maranta
leuconeura
Kerchoveana

Ficus diversifolia

Tradescantia
albiflora

Episcia
cupreata

Caladium
humboldtii

Anthurium
scherzerianum

High-light plants are plants growing in south windows or in rooms that have skylights—in other words, rooms that are sunlit most of the day. The strongest source of high light is a south window that is not obstructed by outdoor shrubbery or nearby buildings. If that location proves to be too sunny for your plants, you can introduce partial shading with sheer curtains or Venetian blinds turned at half-mast. Some high-light plants for terrariums include:

Cacti	Dionaea	Serissa
Cuphea	Iresine	Succulents
Cymbalaria	Oxalis	Trifolium
Dichondra	Sarracenia	

Cuphea hyssopifolia

Dionaea muscipula

Serissa foetida variegata

Oxalis hedysaroides rubra

Crassula schmidtii

Astrophytum myriostigma

Dichondra repens

growing temperatures

Warm-temperature plants grow at a temperature range of 65° to 90° F. The minimum temperature is the most critical for these plants. Tissue damage occurs if temperature drops much below the minimum. A 10° temperature drop at night is beneficial when plants such as those listed below are grown in the upper register of this range.

Acorus	Episcia	Philodendron
Aglaonema	Ferns, tropical	Pilea
Anthurium	Ficus	Pistia
Aphelandra	Fittonia	Saintpaulia
Caladium	Hydrocleys	Scindapsus
Calathea	Maranta	Sinningia
Chamaedorea	Mimosa	Spathiphyllum
Cryptanthus	Nepenthes	Streptocarpus
Dichorisandra	Pellionia	Syngonium
Dracaena	Peperomia	

The Terrarium Book

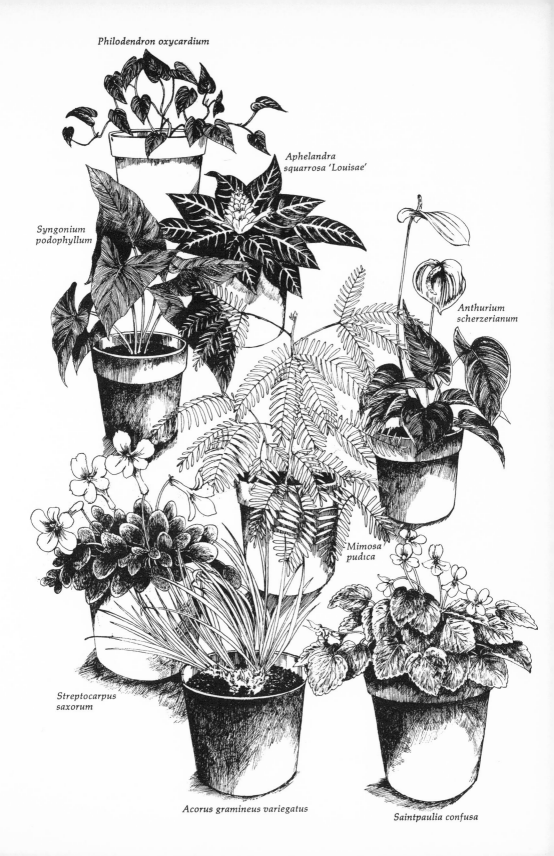

Philodendron oxycardium

Aphelandra squarrosa 'Louisae'

Syngonium podophyllum

Anthurium scherzerianum

Mimosa pudica

Streptocarpus saxorum

Acorus gramineus variegatus

Saintpaulia confusa

Intermediate-temperature plants will thrive at temperatures ranging from 50° to 75° F. The temperature range for these plants is quite large, but they must be kept on the cool side in the winter. The following plants also enjoy a 10° night-time drop:

Ajuga	Hydrocotyle	Rosa
Allophyton	Iresine	Rosemarinus
Ardisia	Lemna	Sansevieria
Arisaema	Myriophyllum	Saxifraga
Buxus	Myrsine	Scilla
Ceropegia	Myrtus	Selaginella
Chlorophytum	Ophiopogon	Streptocarpus
Cuphea	Oxalis	Tradescantia
Dichondra	Pittosporum	Zebrina
Helxine	Podocarpus	

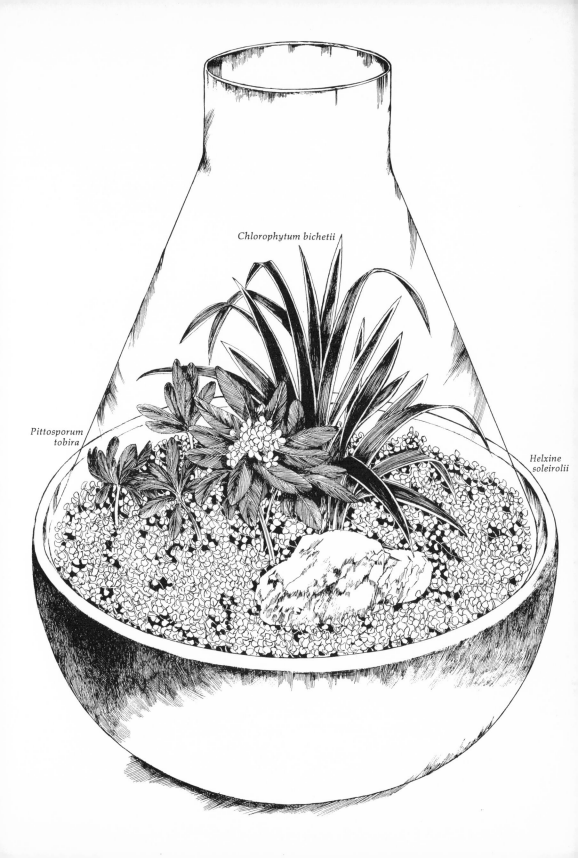

Chlorophytum bichetii

*Pittosporum
tobira*

*Helxine
soleirolii*

Cool-temperature plants must be grown in the low temperature range of 35° to 65° F. Plants in this category need a winter temperature within this range, preferably in the lower register. The following plants will survive higher temperatures, but if possible, try to hold them no higher than a 65° maximum.

Cymbalaria	Hedera	Osmanthus
Darlingtonia	Marchantia	Sarracenia
Dionaea	Mitchella	Serissa
Drosera	Nasturtium	Trifolium
Euonymus	Nertera	

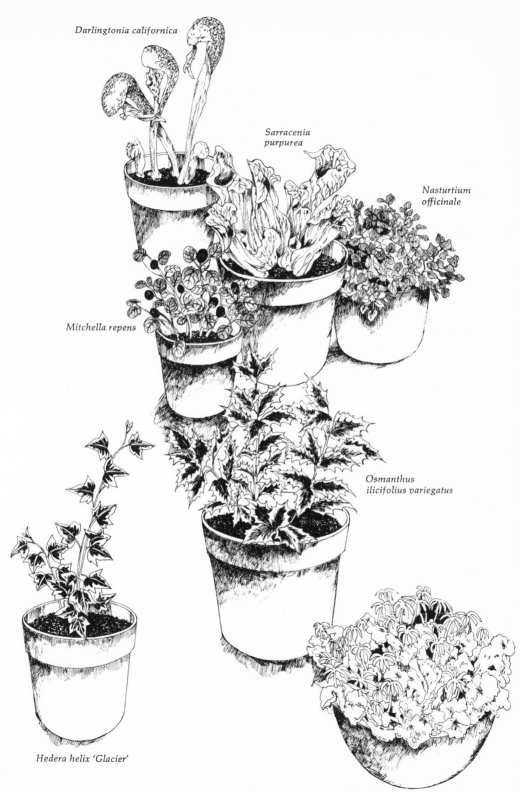

Darlingtonia californica

Sarracenia purpurea

Nasturtium officinale

Mitchella repens

Osmanthus ilicifolius variegatus

Hedera helix 'Glacier'

Marchantia polymorpha

plants for closed containers

Most of the plants listed below not only will grow in permanently closed containers, but they actually need the intense humidity and protected environment of a closed container. In Florida, Drosera (Sundew) and Dionaea (Venus-flytrap) are grown in closed terrariums even in greenhouses.

Ajuga	Dracaena	Maranta
Allophyton	Drosera	Marchantia
Anthurium	Episcia	Nasturtium
Caladium	Ferns	Oxalis
Calathea	Fittonia	Philodendron
Chamaedorea	Goodyera	Selaginella
Dionaea	Helxine	Streptocarpus

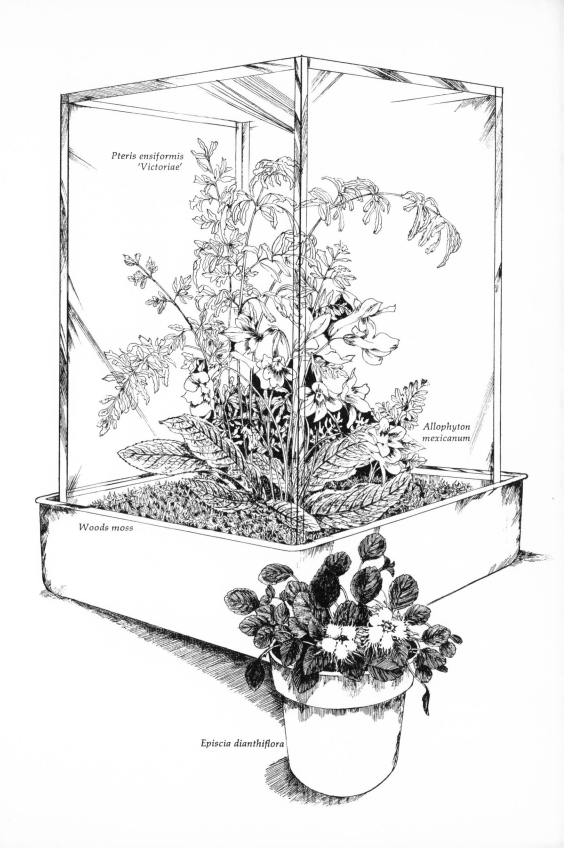

Pteris ensiformis 'Victoriae'

Allophyton mexicanum

Woods moss

Episcia dianthiflora

plants needing ventilation

The following plants must be grown in well-ventilated terrariums, and care should be exercised to avoid over-watering. The soggy atmosphere of a closed, humid terrarium will cause these plants to develop bacterial and fungus diseases. Cacti and succulent terrariums should be left permanently open; the other plants will thrive if the terrarium is opened on a regular basis, perhaps for a couple of hours every day or for longer periods of time every other day.

Cacti and	Mitchella	Pilea
succulents	Myrtus	Rosa
Ceropegia	Pellionia	Rosmarinus
Cuphea	Peperomia	Saintpaulia
Mimosa		

Rosmarinus officinalis

Pellionia daveauana

Tropical plants include many of the familiar house plants that good garden stores and mail-order suppliers regularly stock. They come in pots, and although you may recognize some of the following only as plants that you've seen very large specimens of, you will be able to find the same specimens in their juvenile forms, which are very small. As they are very slow growers, these babies will thrive nicely in relatively little space for quite some time. Tropical plants come in a huge variety of appearances and you can create all sorts of illusions using them exclusively. If you like miniatures, there are tiny creepers and dainty little flowering plants with which you can create an entire garden in a four-inch-square terrarium. If your fancy runs to a wild tropical jungle look, you have an enormous variety of plants to choose from. Some of the following, such as Osmanthus (sweet olive), Rosa (miniature rose) and Iresine (bloodleaf), make good single-plant terrarium subjects, with a bit of moss or pebbles covering the soil surface to give a finished look. Others, such as Ficus (fig), Philodendron and Hedera (ivy), will clamber up the terrarium walls. Whatever you choose, do remember that culture for all the plants in one container must be similiar. Here is a selection:

Aglaonema	Ferns, tropical	Pilea
Allophyton	Ficus	Rosa
Aphelandra	Fittonia	Saintpaulia
Ardisia	Hedera	Sansevieria
Buxus	Iresine	Scilla
Caladium	Maranta	Scindapsus
Calathea	Mimosa	Serissa
Ceropegia	Myrsine	Sinningia
Cryptanthus	Myrtus	Spathiphyllum
Cuphea	Ophiopogon	Stenotaphrum
Cymbalaria	Osmanthus	Streptocarpus
Dichondra	Oxalis	Syngonium
Dichorisandra	Pellonia	Tradescantia
Episcia	Peperomia	Trifolium
Euonymus	Philodendron	Zebrina

Calathea micans

Aglaonema sp.

Ceropegia woodii

Iresine herbstii

Zebrina pendula

Sansevieria trifasciata 'Hahnii'

Woodland plants are sometimes available commercially. Although woods plants grow in a variety of locations, the soil mixtures recommended for these plants will suit both store-bought and outdoor-collected plants. There are many plants you might collect in local woods. However, check with your local conservation societies or government conservation agents, for some plants are endangered species. When you do collect plants from the woods, remember that small pieces will root easily in the terrarium. In addition, it would be nice if you collected only plants that appear to be growing fairly abundantly and if you replant those you may have accidentally uprooted. A trowel or a large soup spoon are useful tools for digging, and plastic food-wrap bags with a bit of water sprinkled inside will keep your treasures alive long enough for you to reach home and plant them in your terrarium. If you are carrying your plants in a car, do not put them near the car heater or in a closed car trunk. They will swelter and die; and all your digging efforts will have gone for naught. The following are some woodland plants:

Arisaema triphyllum (Jack-in-the-pulpit)
Campanula rotundifolia (bluebell)
Chimaphila sp. (pipsissewa)
Claytonia virginica (spring beauty)
Epigaea repens (trailing arbutus)

Equisetum sp.   *Trillium sp.*   *Epigaea repens*   *Myosotis lara*

Equisetum sp. (horsetails)
Ferns, woodland
Gaultheria procumbens (checkerberry)
Goodyera pubescens (rattlesnake plantain)
Lichens
Lycopodiums (princess pine)
Mitchella repens (partridge berry)
Moss
Myosotis lara (forget-me-not)
Polygonatum biflorum (Solomon's seal)
Seedlings of evergreen and deciduous trees
Trillium sp. (dwarf wakerobin)
Viola sp. (wild violets)

Polygonaum biflorum

Campanula rotundifolia

Chimaphila sp.

Goodyera pubescens

Viola sp.

Claytonia virginica

Bog and carnivorous plants create the most dramatic terrariums. Long considered horticultural curiosities, the carnivorous plants are well known to science-fiction-movie devotees as cannibalistic monsters. However, the movie-screen horrors are actually blow-ups of small, harmless, quite exotically shaped and colored plant oddities that in nature are found in bogs and swamps. Some, properly termed insectivorous (they eat insects, not animals), trap live flies and mosquitoes. If these are not available, bits of ground meat will keep them happy and serve to amuse you as you watch the plants open their "jaws" and snap-up their "prey."

Most of the insect-eaters are perfect terrarium subjects because they need extremely high humidity; in fact, they will not survive outside a terrarium. Although they grow in bogs, do be careful not to overwater. Soil should be constantly moist but not waterlogged. It is particularly important in this type of terrarium to use distilled water or rain water. The salt and chlorine content of processed water is especially damaging to bog plants.

Do not overfeed carnivorous plants. Use minute crumbs of lean hamburger very sparingly, because excess food that plants cannot digest will rot and form plant-damaging bacteria. Try not to feed them more than once or twice a month. If plants obviously droop or do not grow at all, use a very dilute solution of an organic fertilizer, such as fish emulsion or cow manure.

Those plants asterisked in the following list are insectivorous plants. The others are water- and bog-loving creepers and trailers that grow in the same conditions as carnivorous plants.

Acorus	Hydrocleys	* Nepenthes
Arisaema	Hydrocotyle	Nertera
Azolla	Lemna	Pistia
* Darlingtonia	Marchantia	Salvinia
* Dionaea	Marsilea	* Sarracenia
* Drosera	Myriophyllum	Spathiphyllum
Hepatica	Nasturtium	

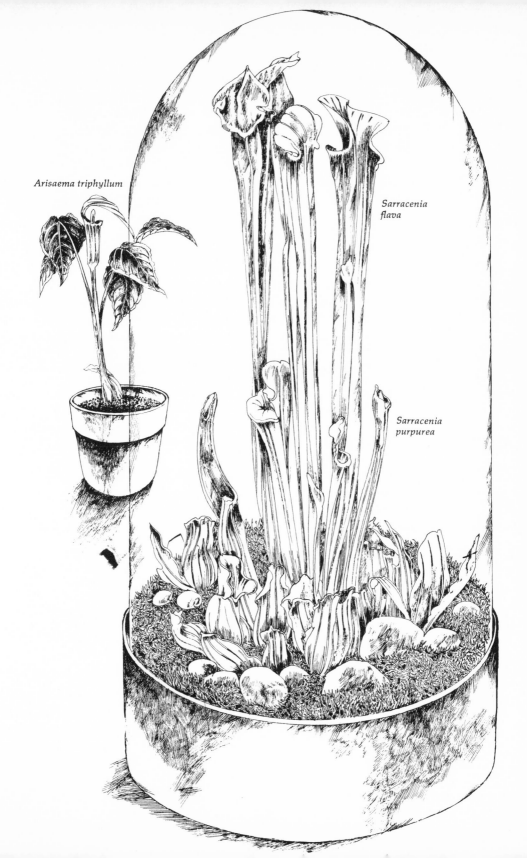

Arisaema triphyllum

Sarracenia flava

Sarracenia purpurea

Cacti and succulents are found in naturally small varieties, and many ordinarily large ones are readily found as seedlings. As nearly all cacti are remarkably slow-growing, anything that looks small enough to fit into the terrarium will remain that way for a long enough time.

Because cacti tend to rather stiff, geometrical shapes, you may wish to soften the design of such a terrarium with small succulents, which come in assorted shades of green, gray and red. Many succulents and most cacti flower if kept cold and dry in winter.

Whatever you choose, remember that most succulents and all desert cacti do *not* want high humidity. You may quite successfully use them in a terrarium, especially the more fragile, delicate succulents, but the terrarium should be the wide-mouthed variety that is always left open. A cacti and succulent terrarium is the one terrarium that must be allowed to dry out periodically. Generally, watering once a week or every ten days is sufficient during the winter; more frequent watering is needed the remainder of the year, but however frequently the terrarium is watered, the soil must be dry before re-watering.

A few small desert cacti include:

> *Lemaireocereus beneckei* (chalk candle)
> *Cephalocereus senilis* (old man cactus)
> *Rathbunia alamosensis* (rambling ranchero)
> *Chamaecereus silvestri* (peanut cactus)
> *Rebutia kupperiana* (red crown)
> *Echinocereus purpureus* (purple hedge hog)
> *Blossfeldia liliputana* (liliput cactus)

Some small succulents of varying colors and textures are:

> *Aloe* sp.
> *Crassula schmidtii* (red-flowering crassula)
> *Crassula 'Marnieriana hybrid'* (jade necklace)
> *Echeveria elegans* (Mexican snowball)
> *Euphorbia pulvinata* (pin-cushion euphorbia)
> *Haworthia papillosa* (pearly dots)
> *Sedum* sp.

The Terrarium Book

Rathbunia alamosensis

Cephalocereus senilis

Chamaecereus silvestri

Rebutia
kupperiana

Aloe variegata

Crassula
'Marnieriana
hybrid'

Haworthia papillosa

Sedum sieboldii

Echinocereus purpureus

Lemaireocereus beneckei

flowering and fruiting plants

If you have good medium light or high light, the following plants will provide your terrarium gardens with lots of color and nearly year-round bloom. The gesneriads (flame violet, dwarf gloxinia and African violet), Ardisia (coral berry), and Spathiphyllum (Spathe flower) bloom intermittently throughout the year.

Allophyton	Episcia	Rosa
Aphelandra	Mitchella	Saintpaulia
Ardisia	Nertera	Sinningia
Ceropegia	Osmanthus	Spathiphyllum
Cuphea	Oxalis	Streptocarpus

Episcia cupreata

Saintpaulia sp.

Sinningia pusilla

ground-cover plants These plants are just what they sound like—plants that cover the ground or, in this case, the soil surface. In conjunction with bushy or treelike plants or vines, they give a finished look to the terrarium. By themselves, they make excellent subjects for the very small terrarium. *Ficus pumila minima* (miniature creeping fig) and the Selaginellas will climb up terrarium walls as well as creep along soil surfaces. *Nertera depressa* (coral-bead plant), with little persimmon-colored berries, and *Ceropegia woodii* (string of hearts), with its tiny, urn-shaped purple flowers and variegated leaves would provide colorful accents for the miniature terrarium.

Azolla caroliniana
Ceropegia woodii
Cymbalaria muralis
Dichondra repens
Euonymus fortunei uncinatus
Ficus pumila minima
Gaultheria procumbens
Helxine soleirolii
Hydrocotyle rotundifolia
Lemna minor
Marchantia polymorpha
Mitchella repens
Nertera depressa
Pellionia daveauana
   P. pulchra
Peperomia prostrata
Polypodium lycopodioides
Salvinia auriculata
Selaginella sp.
Trifolium repens minus

The Terrarium Book

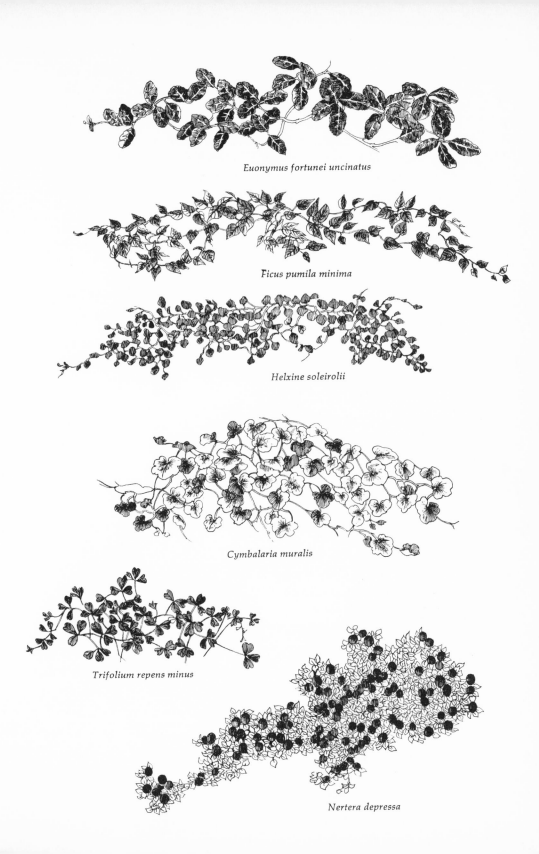

Euonymus fortunei uncinatus

Ficus pumila minima

Helxine soleirolii

Cymbalaria muralis

Trifolium repens minus

Nertera depressa

ferns (tropical) Ferns are perhaps the most traditional of terrarium plants, if only because it was a fern that unexpectedly sprouted and grew in the first unplanned Wardian case a hundred and fifty years ago. Now, with central heating and air conditioning robbing most homes of the humidity that ferns need, they are still most successfully cultivated under glass. Collectors can scout plant shops and mail-order catalogs to create tropical fern gardens in terrarium containers. Others may prefer to use ferns in combination with woodland plants or other tropicals that grow in similiar conditions. Several good terrarium subjects are listed below. (In general, look for miniature varieties, as ferns can be rapid growers under optimal conditions. Fertilizing should be infrequent, organic and highly diluted.)

Adiantum	Pellaea	Pteris
Azolla	Polypodium	Salvinia
Marsilea		

Pteris cretica

Pellaea rotundifolia

Polypodium polypodioides

Mosses are found in many varieties that one can collect from the woods, but they often serve as nurseries for evergreen seedlings. Mosses are best collected and carried home in plastic bags, with the tops tied or taped shut. Do not put them in the car trunk or near the car heater. Some interesting varieties that grow nearly everywhere and that can also be purchased from terrarium suppliers are:

Aulacomnium heterostichum (furrowed moss)
Bartramia pomiformis (apple moss)
Dicranum scoparium (broom moss)
Leucobryum glaucum (pin-cushion moss)

Lichens almost defy description. Composed of algae and fungi, the lichens are multi-shaped and multi-colored formations that coat the surfaces of rocks and tree bark, somewhat like ship barnacles. They can also be found on old, rotting wood posts and fences. They will not grow in polluted air, so you have to look for them way out in the country. Most tend to be olive-green or gray, which contrasts quite nicely with brighter-colored terrarium plants. (In some places, particularly in the Southwest, one can find lichens in bright colors.) They may grow rampantly in terrariums, so it would be wise to plant very little to start with.

Woodland ferns are grown under the same conditions as tropical ferns. Some, such as the small maidenhair types, are quite similiar to tropicals. The deciduous varieties should be collected before first frost, but evergreens may be acquired at any time. As with the collection of any woodland plants, do not be selfish or too acquisitive in your plant collecting. They will grow well and multiply in a terrarium garden, and you do not want to upset the ecology any more than necessary. A few common deciduous varieties are:

4/
Soils

With your container and plants decided on, your next project is to determine what kind of soil you will need. It's probably not overstating the case to say that good or bad soil can make or break a terrarium. It happens that many quite diverse plants have the same or very similar soil requirements, just as many different plants have similar light requirements. That is why, in a terrarium or any planting situation, you can group different plants together. The point here is to determine the elements that go into mixing a good soil and to know which of several basic types of soil mixtures is right for different groups of plants.

Because terrariums by their very nature have no drainage holes, a well-textured terrarium soil must be porous enough for good water drainage and air exchange. If plant roots are deprived of oxygen, they will die, and without drainage holes to release excess water, soil easily becomes waterlogged. However, if the soil is porous, it will allow oxygen-bearing air to pass through and reach plant roots.

What you need to do is to assemble a well-textured, nourishing soil mixture for your terrarium planting. Garden topsoil or packaged potting soil will do as a start for the terrarium soil mix, but both have to be supported by several other soil components to ensure porosity, retain sufficient moisture, and provide nourishment and enough firmness to hold plants in place.

If you use soil from your garden, sterilize it first to prevent fungus, weed, bacterial and insect growth. To sterilize, spread soil out thinly in flat pans (pie plates or roasting pans) and bake at 200° for three hours. Higher temperatures will burn out organic nutrients in the soil.

If you buy potting soil, ask for the sterilized variety.

soil components

Listed here are the kinds of soil components used in terrariums. Specific instructions for their mixture for various kinds of planting follow below.

Garden topsoil varies in composition, ranging from sandy to heavy clay. A clay-based soil that tends to pack and usually contains weed seed and organic matter is the most common. Sterilize to kill weed seed. Add peat, perlite and sand to provide the porosity necessary to good drainage and air exchange.

Standard potting soil (sometimes sold as planting or house-plant soil) is a packaged soil that tends to be heavy-textured, muddy when first watered and powdery when dry. Soil particles do not cling well and, in a dry state, may not hold plants upright.

Sandy potting soil (also sold as cactus soil) is usually a standard potting soil with some sand added. It is a good base for mixing a terrarium soil, because it is not too rich in nutrients. Add peat and perlite, and it will adequately serve a wide variety of terrarium plants.

Black Magic Planter Mix is a commercial preparation

composed of a variety of organic materials that include almost everything one might use in a soil mixture except soil itself. Alone it is overtextured for terrariums, but added in equal parts to sandy soil, it makes an excellent terrarium mix.

Perlite is expanded volcanic rock with no nutritive value per se, but its lightweight particles allow good drainage and aeration in heavy soil. However, it may make the soil mix too lightweight to hold plants upright, particularly if the soil base is already light-textured. This situation can be corrected by reducing the amount of perlite or by adding some sand.

Vermiculite is expanded mica that also has no nutritive value and is often confused with perlite. However, unlike perlite, it does not provide drainage but retains moisture and soluble nutrients.

Peat moss that is commercially available is decomposed sphagnum moss. As it further decomposes in a soil mixture, it releases nutrients that stimulate growth from root hairs and acidify the soil mix. Wet peat moss has a spongy texture that deters soil from compacting and helps retain moisture without waterlogging. It is important to moisten peat moss thoroughly before adding it to soil mixtures. As it absorbs water slowly in its dry state, the easiest way to moisten it is to pour boiling water through it. Wait until it cools off and then wring it out or drain off excess water.

Sphagnum moss is an undecomposed bog moss that is sold dehydrated in milled or shredded forms and in a long-strand form. The shredded form is easiest to use; it should be moistened like peat moss before adding it to soil mixes. It provides aeration, drainage, water retention and nutrients that are good for plant roots.

Sand is a useful addition to any soil mix, because it contributes to drainage, air circulation, grit and friability. You need sharp sand that feels abrasive when rubbed between your fingers.

Humus, or **leafmold,** is decayed vegetable matter that provides an organic source of nutrients to plants. Like peat, although to a lesser degree, it tends to acidify soil mixes. Humus is the completely decomposed form of leafmold.

Charcoal, the horticultural variety, can be purchased in crushed form from garden stores. It absorbs soil impurities and adds porosity. Mixed with soil and distributed among drainage material, it will absorb the rank odor of decomposing material and keep terrariums sweet-smelling.

Grit is rough sand or fine gravel; aquarium gravel or bird gravel are good examples. Grit promotes root-hair growth and adds to soil porosity.

Moss lining, used sometimes in terrariums to conceal the soil structure, should be live, growing moss that you peel from rocks and bark. This is the best kind, because it grows in thin layers and will continue to grow within the terrarium, so that your entire planting appears to rise out of a bed of moss.

how to mix your soil Soil components should be thoroughly mixed and well dampened, but not soaked, before planting. For each terrarium choose plants that have the same soil and care requirements. Several mixtures are given for each category of planting. Choose the formula that you feel most comfortable with or that is composed of materials you already have on hand. (When we refer to sandy soil or standard potting soil, we mean the packaged mix.)

The Terrarium Book

Peat Moss (handwritten)

For tropical plantings:

Mix 1: 2 parts sandy soil
1 part peat moss
1 part perlite

Mix 2: 2 parts garden soil or standard potting soil
1 part peat moss
1 part perlite
1 part sand

Mix 3: 1 part Black Magic
1 part sand
2 parts standard potting soil or garden soil

For woodland plantings:

Mix 1: 2 parts humus
1 part sand
2 parts peat moss
1 part perlite

Mix 2: 1 part sphagnum moss
2 parts humus
1 part perlite
1 part peat moss

Mix 3: 1 part Black Magic
1 part sandy soil

For cacti and succulent plantings:

Mix 1: 3 parts sandy soil
2 parts humus
1 part perlite
1 part charcoal
1 part grit (fine gravel)

Mix 2: 2 parts Black Magic
1 part sandy soil
1 part grit

For carnivorous and bog plantings:

Mix 1: 3 parts peat moss
2 parts potting soil
1 part charcoal
1 part sand

Mix 2: Live sphagnum moss on top of bed of peat moss

drainage materials

Now that you have a well-drained soil, you have to provide for excess water. In a flower pot, this will seep out of drainage holes, but in a terrarium, the soil must rest on a layer of drainage material from one-half to two inches deep, depending on the size of the terrarium. Mix three parts gravel to one part charcoal for the drainage layer, to catch excess water and hold it until it evaporates.

The size of the pieces of gravel should be proportionate to the size of the terrarium. Pebbles should be large enough to allow air space between individual pieces to hold water. Pea gravel suits large tank-type cases, whereas aquarium gravel is more in scale with very small terrariums. Aquarium gravel is the smallest gradation that can provide drainage; if your terrarium is really too tiny even for that, you can skip the drainage layer. But you must then be most careful not to overwater.

Marble chips or other calciferous rocks should not be used for drainage, because they will slowly cause the soil to become alkaline. You can use beach or river pebbles or clear glass marbles. Pebbles are expensive to buy but it's fun to collect them yourself from the beach or the woods. Glass marbles are available in quarter-, half-, and three-quarter-inch sizes. Unlike the way it used to be, they are now hard to find but when you do locate them, they can be purchased in large quantities fairly inexpensively.

A soil separator is essential in terrariums because it prevents soil from washing down into the drainage area as the terrarium is watered. Without it, drainage would soon look dirty and, more important, it would become clogged and unable to serve its water-collecting function.

Use fiberglass, plastic fine-grade screening, fine nylon netting, old nylon stockings or sheet moss (though this will eventually decompose). Place the separator material in one thin layer between the soil and the pebbles or gravel or marbles of your drainage level.

soil separators

Rocks and large pebbles, collected from the woods, the beach, your backyard or even construction sites can be used for landscaping the terrarium. If the terrarium is relatively large, rocks and such will help to bank and mound the soil, so the terrarium can be planted on split- or multi-levels. Small pieces of slate, broken bricks, pieces of old wood, or volcanic feather rock can also aid in securing multi-levels or simply adding decorative effects to the terrarium landscape.

decorative materials

Be sure to wash all rocks and pebbles or whatever else you collect before using them in the terrarium. The salt clinging to unwashed beach pebbles, for example, makes them unhealthy for terrarium plantings. Other decorative matter may have assorted impurities that you wouldn't want to introduce into your planting.

Pteris cretica

Calathea makoyana

Moss

5/
Planting

You have assembled a container, some plants, a good soil mixture, drainage material, a soil separator, moss lining and perhaps some decorative objects—all the ingredients needed to set up a terrarium. Now what do you do with all these things? Which goes in first, and where, and how?

Before you begin, think about terrarium gardening as a step-by-step procedure whose principles are much the same as those of pot or outdoor gardening, except that you are planting within glass walls. As in cooking, each step prepares the way for the next step until you arrive at the finished product.

preparing the container

The interior of the terrarium must be clean before so much as one pebble is dropped in. You will find it really difficult to clean after planting is completed. Glass cleaner wiped on and off with a soft cloth will do for normal soiling; bleach, coffeepot cleaner, toilet-bowl cleaner or rust remover will eradicate stubborn stains. Never use abrasive cleaners or steel wool on glass.

placing the drainage material

Before putting the drainage material and the soil mixture in the terrarium, decide whether you want the layers to show through the sides or whether you want to line the container with live moss, the green side facing out, so that the soil structure is concealed and the planting will appear to be growing in a bed of moss.

The amount of drainage to use should be based on a ratio of about one-half inch of drainage for every inch of soil, up to about two inches of drainage. If you're planting an extremely small terrarium, you may eliminate drainage material, particularly if you're worried about fitting everything in. However, you must then be extremely careful about watering; you will have no margin for error.

Drainage material is always composed of one-fourth charcoal and three-fourths gravel. Wash or sift the charcoal so that its fine dust will not coat the terrarium walls. Gravel size should be proportionate to the size of the terrarium. For containers with small openings the drainage material and soil mixture should be poured through wide-mouthed funnels (typing paper rolled into shape makes a good funnel).

After the drainage material is evenly distributed along the bottom of the terrarium, cover the material with the soil separator.

adding soil

Dampen the soil, but do not soak. Pick up a handful of soil and squeeze it. If it feels moist and falls apart when you relax your hand, and if no water drips between your fingers, then the dampness is just right. For a narrow-necked container, soil may be dry, because it's easier to pour through the narrow opening.

Place the soil in the terrarium, distributing it evenly over the soil separator or banking and mounding, as you prefer. You can slope the soil structure away from the glass walls as a precaution if you anticipate overwatering. Use a soil-moving tool to distribute soil evenly and/or to slope.

The Terrarium Book

The soil should be deep enough to allow for adequate root growth and to hold roots in place. As a rule of thumb, the soil mixture should be about two-thirds of the soil structure, and the entire soil structure should comprise no more than one-fourth of the depth of the terrarium. At least one-half inch of soil would be necessary for even the smallest terrarium. A twelve-inch-high terrarium would have three inches of soil structure, one inch for drainage and the remaining two inches for soil mixture. However, you may vary your proportions somewhat to suit individual circumstances. For example, in a four-inch-high terrarium, the soil structure could be approximately one inch—that is, one-half inch drainage and one-half-inch soil. Sloping will provide a deeper soil layer for plants that have more substantial root systems.

As you work, try to keep the sides of the glass clean. Wipe off smudges as you go; as we said before, the terrarium walls will be much harder to clean after planting is completed.

Generally the terrarium will be more interesting and effective if planting is designed to resemble nature. Rather than just putting your plants into a flat soil bed, try to vary the topography. With pieces of slate or odd-shaped rocks, you can create the effect of mountains and valleys, of rocky slopes and mesas. Space your plants to get the effect of dense woods and open meadows. Or create a small rock garden, using pebbles and broken bricks to secure the various levels as well as to provide decorative effect. The charm of even a single-plant terrarium can be enhanced by the addition of small ground-cover plants around the base of the main plant. **building the terrain**

Assemble all your plants, with whatever decorative extras you've decided to use. Before removing the plants from **arranging the plants**

Planting

their pots, arrange and rearrange them with rocks and pebbles or whatever, until you have a rough idea of your overall design. If you think it might help, you can also sketch a master plan to follow while you're setting in the plants.

wide-mouthed container planting

1. Consider the overall arrangement of your plants and make depressions in the soil where plants are to be placed. Start with the larger plants first, because they need more room and you'll have to dig around much more to get them in. If you leave the larger plant to the end, you may wind up disrupting all the other plants just to accommodate that one.

2. Working slowly and gently, remove some soil from just below the crown (the base) of the plant, and very gently disentangle the bottom roots. Retain as much of the root ball as possible and replant into terrarium soil at exactly the same depth at which the plant was previously growing. You will see a soil line on the crown of any plant, except for ground covers that just skim the soil.

3. After all the plants are in, tamp the soil down over the root balls. Cover the bare-soil areas with moss, ground covers or pebbles. Ground covers or a thin layer of pebbles, besides being pretty and contributing to the landscape effect, help to conserve moisture in the soil by reducing the rate of evaporation.

4. Now water slowly and evenly, distributing water over the entire terrarium. Stop from time to time as you water and wait a few moments to see if the soil turns dark all the way through. If it does, stop watering; if it does not, add more water.

5. Mist the foliage, cover the terrarium, and place in a suitable light.

narrow-necked container planting

1. It is especially important in a bottle garden to dig holes in the soil where plants are to be placed; these should be deep enough to accommodate most of the root mass. Use a digging tool (page 70) for making holes.

The Terrarium Book

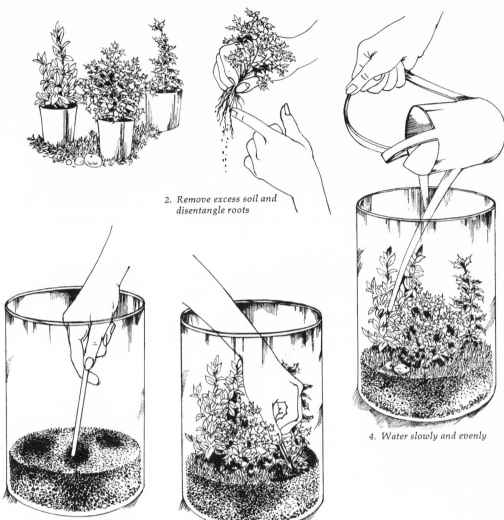

2. Remove excess soil and
disentangle roots

4. Water slowly and evenly

1. Dig holes for plants

3. Insert plants and tamp down soil
over root balls

2. Remove most or all of the soil from the roots. This
is different from ordinary gardening practice because of
the problems of getting a plant of a certain size through
an opening that looks much too small—though chances
are that it's not. You can remove soil from the root ball
by washing the roots under a slow cool faucet. Besides
making it easier to fit the root system through the bottle
neck, washing off roots assures that you will not add more

Planting

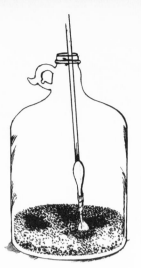

1. *Dig holes in soil for plants*

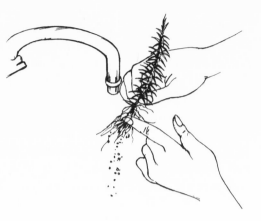

2. *Remove soil from roots*

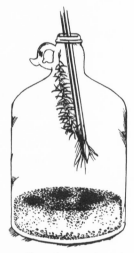

3. *Place plants in the soil*

4. *Cover bare soil*

5. *Clean leaves and bottle*

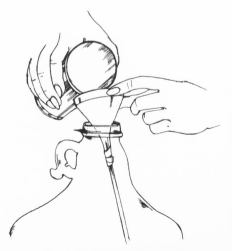

6. *Water with funnel*

soil to the bottle than is needed and prevents soil particles from falling on leaves of plants previously placed in the bottle. While planting, do not allow bare roots to dry out.

3. Lower the plant into the bottle, spread out its roots, and distribute soil in and around and over the root mass, being careful to preserve the original soil level and to tamp soil down. Since you are planting bare-root, keep in mind that the plant needs enough soil around its roots not only to nourish it but to hold it upright. Use the tweezers or a similar gadget, and watch that you don't squeeze the plant too hard and break off its main stem. Take care also not to disturb plants previously planted.

4. After all the plants are in place, cover the bare-soil areas with moss, gravel or other ground covers.

5. Brush or shake soil particles off leaves with either a long stick or a long-handled artist's brush. Clean the soil and smudges off the glass with a bit of sponge on a flexible wire or some damp paper towel on a stick.

6. Trickle water very slowly over the entire planting area, using a funnel and straw. In future waterings you will trickle water down the sides of the bottle, but this first time you must take care to soak the soil, because you started with dry soil. Add the water slowly, allowing time for percolation through the soil. To avoid overwatering, keep adding water until the soil looks moist (dark) all the way through or until the drainage area fills with water. Aquarium tubing manipulated from a bottle serves well as a siphon device for watering because you can pinch the tubing to control the flow. Use aquarium tubing also to siphon off excess water if you happen to overwater your bottle garden.

tools for all kinds of terrariums

Searching for tools and tool parts or inventing your own gadgetry can be an interesting exercise in serendipity. Stores where any of the following tools can be found include auto-supply houses, pet or aquarium shops, variety stores, plumbing suppliers and hardware stores.

Planting

69

Soil-moving tools

Large-necked funnel for inserting drainage material
and soil
Spoon taped to the end of a dowel, dowel with one
end carved into a spatula; chopsticks; a parfait
spoon—all for digging holes and distributing soil
The wrong end of a knitting needle, or a cork
attached to a dowel, for tamping soil

Plant-manipulating tools

Long-handled barbecue or fondue forks
Pick-up tools (sometimes called grabbers), sold in
hardware or auto-supply stores and used for
picking up things that fall into inaccessible places
Coat-hanger wire looped at one end
Long-handled tweezers, taped if the ends are sharp
Aquarium tongs

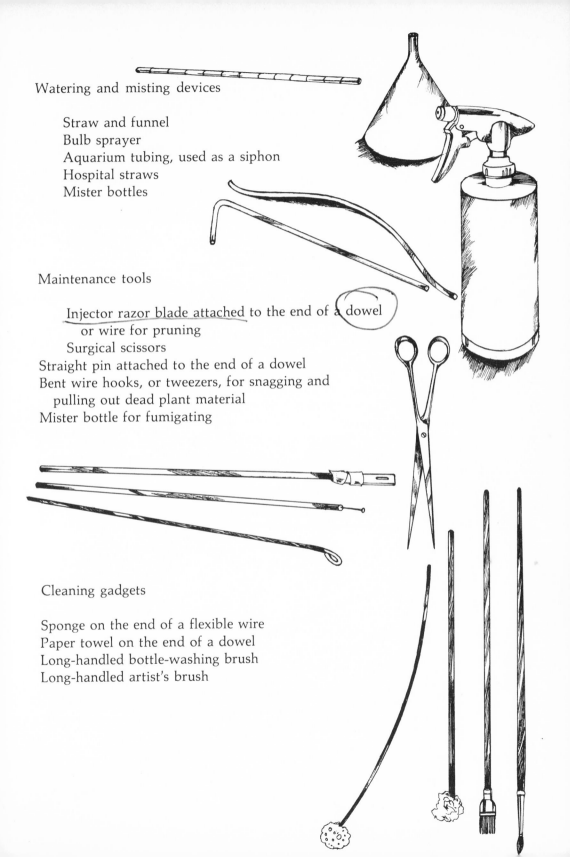

Watering and misting devices

Straw and funnel
Bulb sprayer
Aquarium tubing, used as a siphon
Hospital straws
Mister bottles

Maintenance tools

Injector razor blade attached to the end of a dowel
or wire for pruning
Surgical scissors
Straight pin attached to the end of a dowel
Bent wire hooks, or tweezers, for snagging and
pulling out dead plant material
Mister bottle for fumigating

Cleaning gadgets

Sponge on the end of a flexible wire
Paper towel on the end of a dowel
Long-handled bottle-washing brush
Long-handled artist's brush

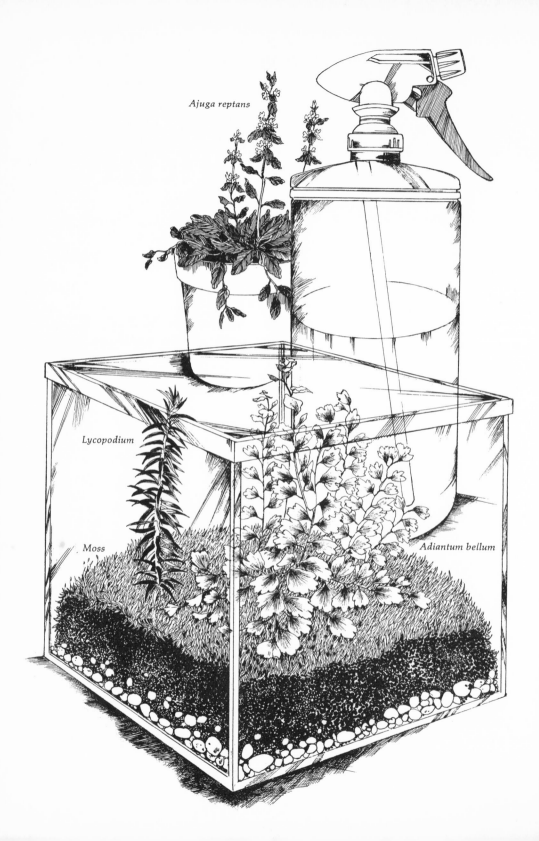

Ajuga reptans

Lycopodium

Moss

Adiantum bellum

6/
Maintenance

At last your terrarium is finished. The plants are in, the glass is clean, the landscaping completed, and the whole effect is as beautiful as you had hoped it would be—perhaps even more so. Now what do you do with it? You don't just put it somewhere and forget about it. Most terrariums will need some attention, but a terrarium ordinarily should require much less in the way of maintenance than a potted-plant collection.

The one terrarium that needs absolutely no attention is the one that has been well planted with slow-growing plants, carefully watered, suitably lighted, made completely insect- and disease-free, and tightly sealed. The average terrarium cannot meet all these requirements, nor should it have to. For one thing, if you really wanted just that type of terrarium, you would be limited to a small selection of plants that could withstand the high humidity of a permanently closed container and that would also grow well in whatever light you were able to provide. On the other hand, if you understand just a few simple principles of keeping up a good terrarium, you can increase the scope of your terrarium gardening quite successfully.

sunlight   Plants tend to lean in the direction of the light source; therefore, you should turn window-sill terrariums around periodically so that your plants will not grow all in one direction. If you keep your terrarium in direct sunlight, there may be an excessive heat build-up, especially in summer. A closed container on a sunny window sill may become hot enough to act as an oven and actually cook the plants.

It is really important that these terrariums be well and frequently ventilated. Remove their covers completely or partially from time to time, and, in summer, partially shade these terrariums. Plants suffering from excess heat will show the results by mild wilting that eventually progresses to death wilt, leaf scorching, shriveling and a general dried-up appearance. Another result of too much sunlight is excessive and frequent moisture condensation on the interior walls of the terrarium and algae growth such as is seen in aquariums; again ventilation and some shading is the solution. A cactus and succulent terrarium is the only type that can be located in full sun with no ill effects.

artificial light   If you do choose plants that will survive low light, keep in mind that low light does *not* mean a dark corner of a room. If that very dark corner is just the place where you think a terrarium would look perfect, then you should consider artificial light. Artificial light, which can be fluorescent, mercury vapor or incandescent light, can be used as a total substitute for natural light or as a supplement to weak natural light. For example, if you live in an apartment building whose view is obstructed by the next building, your window light, no matter which direction it comes from, will be considerably reduced. Mounting an incandescent flood lamp near such a window will considerably increase the total amount of light received by plants on or next to that window sill.

As a total light source for terrariums, fluorescent lamps are probably your best choice. Fluorescent fixtures can be mounted directly above terrariums and can be incorporated in all sorts of decorating schemes, including bookshelves, counter-tops, above and below tables, on top of or underneath extended window sills—the possibilities are limited only by your space and taste. For terrariums the best fluorescent lamps are the new color-corrected tubes. These produce a full spectrum light, which is necessary for all growing plants, and they do not cast that objectionable purple glow usually associated with fluorescent plant lighting.

The length of the light fixture and the number of its tubes will pretty well determine whether you can grow low-, medium- or high-light plants under it. For example, a two-lamp, twenty-four-inch fixture will suffice for low-light plants. Increasing the number of lamps and/or the length of the fixture will produce higher light suitable for medium- and high-light plants. Moving the lamps closer to or away from the fixture can vary the light intensity, but in no case should the terrarium plants be any further from the fluorescent tubes than eighteen inches.

Plants, like people, need to sleep—that is, they need about eight hours of darkness a day (or night, as you prefer). Flowering plants want somewhat less than twelve hours of light a day during their dormant periods; foliage plants and blooming plants on the average will grow nicely with about fourteen to sixteen hours a day of light. Use a timing device to ensure that your plants receive light and darkness at consistent, regular intervals.

Incandescent lighting (photo flood lamps and ordinary table and floor lamps) should be used for terrariums only as supplementary lighting where natural light is inadequate. Color-corrected mercury vapor lamps, those designed for growing plants, may be used quite successfully as a total light source for terrariums. These lamps transmit considerable heat and they should be placed about three to seven feet above the plants.

Maintenance

watering　If your terrarium is permanently closed and was properly watered after planting was completed, a moisture-recycling process takes place that relieves you of all further responsibility for this chore. As moisture evaporates from the soil and is transpired by plant leaves, it condenses on the interior terrarium walls and in turn runs down into the soil again. If your terrarium is uncovered, or requires regular ventilation, or if your planting consists of young specimens, you will have to water it from time to time, though much less often than you would an equivalent collection of potted plants.

Chlorine and soluble salts, both of which exist in the ordinary tap water of many localities, can play havoc with terrariums. You can solve the chlorine problem by allowing tap water to stand overnight in an open container; the chlorine will dissipate in that time. Salt will not evaporate. In flower pots, salt is leached out as water leaks out through drainage holes; in clay pots, salt is also absorbed by the clay, giving old pots their characteristic white coating. In a terrarium, there's nowhere that salt can go except into the soil. Therefore, it's really best to water the terrarium with distilled water, rain water, or melted snow—all at room temperature. You can buy distilled water at supermarkets or drugstores.

Do not pour all the water in one place, especially in a large terrarium, but rather water lightly and evenly over the entire planting surface. A mister, rather than a watering can, is good for light watering, especially for very small terrariums. But be generous when using a mister, for it yields much less water than a watering can. A mister may not be sufficient for a well-ventilated or open terrarium or one that has been allowed to dry out too thoroughly. The mister, in such cases, may still prove a useful supplement to the watering can as a way to raise humidity or clean foliage. A funnel can serve as a watering device for very narrow-necked bottles. You move the funnel so that water trickles down the sides of the container to avoid disturbing the planting.

The Terrarium Book

When to water is a much trickier problem than how to water. If the terrarium opening is large enough for you to put your hand in, then the finger method used for potted plants is easy and accurate. Stick your forefinger down about an inch or so below the soil surface. If it feels perceptibly damp, withhold water. If dry, water immediately. Terrariums should not be allowed to dry out, so it's important to notice that your terrarium needs watering before it becomes completely dry. If you've planted a terrarium with a narrow opening, you will simply have to observe when to water. Watering is indicated if plants appear limp, soil looks light-colored, and there are no beads of moisture on interior walls of terrarium. If you pick up your terrarium before and after watering the first few times, you will be able to tell after a while just by lifting it in the palm of your hand whether it is heavy and hefty with moisture or lightweight because it has dried out. Good gardeners do this all the time with potted plants.

Some people worry too much about such things and tend to overwater plants the way some people overfeed their children. Overwatering can be even worse for plants than underwatering. The exchange of gases—oxygen and carbon dioxide—necessary for plant health is effected by the watering process. When a plant is watered, the water takes up air spaces between soil particles and drives out carbon dioxide. When that water is absorbed by plant roots and soil and finally evaporated, air returns to soil spaces, pulling in oxygen with it. If there is too much water or if watering is too frequent, the root zone becomes waterlogged, roots rot away, and plants decay and finally die. If you have poured in too much water, it will be obvious; the drainage area will fill with water and the top of the soil will become waterlogged. You must siphon the extra water off, sponge it up, or soak it up any way you can without disturbing the planting. Do not tip the terrarium over to drain out excess water! Even plants that grow in water should not be waterlogged in a terrarium, for the still water in a terrarium tends to stagnate.

humidity and ventilation

One would suppose that a terrarium is the one growing situation where lack of humidity would be no problem (except for Foggy Bottom in midsummer). However, if the terrarium is too frequently ventilated or usually left uncovered, central heating in winter might reduce its humidity to an unhealthy level for most terrarium plants, particularly ferns and mosses that will survive nowhere else indoors except in closed terrariums. All terrariums should show some moisture condensation on their walls. If it is absent, then humidity is too low.

In a permanently or usually corked or covered container, humidity might become excessive—a condition made obvious by dense moisture condensation, molds and rotting leaves. In that case, ventilate the terrarium. Excessive humidity can produce the same unhappy results that you get from overwatering. If you think you've overwatered and have not been able to remove enough water by the recommended methods, leaving the terrarium uncovered for a day or two will speed up evaporation.

fertilizing

With the optimal growing conditions provided by the terrarium environment, the last thing terrarium plants might seem to need would be fertilizer, particularly if you are anxious that your planting remain where it is as long as possible. However, living plants are not stable; they either grow or degenerate. Even with the good growing atmosphere of a well-maintained terrarium, plants will grow and use up nutrients in the soil, and need some minimal feeding if growth is to be strong and healthy.

Use fertilizer diluted to one-quarter of the manufacturer's instructions and no more than half as often as he recommends or as you are accustomed to feeding potted plants. Or you can mix into your soil a small amount of bone meal or dry cow manure, which are slow-dissolving organic fertilizers. If you are even slightly in doubt as to how much fertilizer to use, use too little rather than too much. The point is to support slow, strong growth, not encourage rapid, weak, leggy growth. Also, without drainage holes, there's no way in a terrarium to leach out salts built up by excessive fertilizing.

temperature

Most terrarium plants will grow quite successfully in an intermediate temperature range of 50° to 85°. All plants grown within this range require a night-time temperature drop of 10°, but it is important that the temperature does not drop below 50° in winter.

Some plants need cooler or warmer temperatures. A cool temperature range is 35° to 65°. Here a slight night-time drop is good, but not essential. In any case, the temperature of the terrarium must not drop below a winter low of 35°.

A warm range is 65° to 90°. Again, the 10° night-time drop is important, always providing that the winter low does not fall below 65°.

Unless the terrarium is placed in direct sunlight, its temperature will be approximately room temperature, but if the terrarium is closed, the glass walls will protect plants from drafts and sudden chilly night-time temperature drops.

insects and diseases

If, before planting, you meticulously examine each plant for insects and apply appropriate remedies if you find any (even if it means throwing the plant out and getting a new one), you're quite unlikely ever to get insects in your terrarium. Once in the terrarium, clean plants are not likely to be infested, especially if the terrarium is closed.

When, despite all precautions, your terrarium is visited by an insect infestation, you must respond immediately. Insects spread quickly and easily; in the small enclosed environment of a terrarium, the infesta-

Maintenance

79

tion can decimate the entire planting. Use a general-purpose aerosol insecticide specifically manufactured for indoor-plant pests, and leave the terrarium closed for an hour or so after spraying in order to fumigate the pests. An aerosol is recommended for terrariums, because hand-mixed sprays and sprayers usually indicated for potted plants are cumbersome in terrariums and frequently one cannot reach the undersides of leaves. An aerosol mist tends to be fine enough to be carried on air currents that reach all parts of the plant. Concentrated insecticides properly diluted may be applied directly, with a small paint brush, to infested areas.

If possible, place sheets of paper between glass walls and plants before spraying; if not, in narrow-necked bottles, wipe the spray off the interior walls. The piece of damp sponge on the end of a flexible wire should serve the purpose in a bottle garden.

Ferns will not tolerate spraying; these plants really must be examined most carefully before planting, and insects have to be picked off ferns by hand. A systemic insecticide, which is easier to use in a terrarium than a spray, will not harm ferns. Systemics come in granular and liquid forms; applied to soil, they are absorbed by the plant, thus protecting its tissues against insect damage.

The following insects and diseases are those you are most likely to encounter in terrariums.

Aphids, one of the most easily controlled plant insects, are about the size of a small ant and come in several colors. They gather around growing tips where they suck plant juices from young, tender tissue. The result is deformed, curled new leaves. They attack practically all plants. An aerosol spray is the best specific remedy.

Mealy bugs are particularly damaging to plants and difficult to eradicate. They look like bits of cotton batten about one-eighth inch long and attach themselves, usually in large numbers, to stems or hide in leaf axes. Begonias, succulents, orchids, palms and soft-stemmed plants are particularly susceptible. Controls include aerosol sprays, systemic poisons or painting with Isotox.

Scale looks like a collection of tiny round mounds or disks that firmly attach themselves to all parts of a plant. They seem to prefer ferns, as well as ivy, palms and some succulents. You can paint the leaves with Malathion or pick off the scale with your fingernail or an eyebrow tweezer. In the case of ferns, do not confuse with fern spores. The scale will pick off easily with your fingernails; the spores will not pull off.

Slugs are gray, inedible, shell-less snails that appear at night and leave shiny slime trails quite visible by day. They tend to hide in moist gravel and eat young, tender plant growth. Either remove and destroy slugs or use slug bait.

Spider mites are nearly invisible to the naked eye but their presence can be detected by the tiny webs they spin on the undersides of leaves and in leaf axes. The damage they cause is swiftly progressive and spectacular; in its advanced stages, a mite infestation causes blotchy, spotty leaves that soon dry up and fall off. Plants sometimes seem to be denuded overnight, but the mites do not give up; they move on to the nearest plant. Ivies are most susceptible; fortunately the humidity in a terrarium is enormously helpful in preventing plants from becoming infested. Controls are aerosol sprays, systemic poisons or painting with Isotox.

White flies are small, snow-white, winged creatures that will fly off a stem or branch if you shake or poke it. The babies suck plant sap, causing plants to turn yellow and limp and eventually to wilt. Coleus, begonias and flowering annuals are the plants most frequently harmed by white flies. Aerosol spray repeated frequently will eradicate these pests.

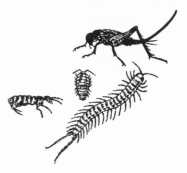

Summer pests such as spiders, crickets, springtails, sow bugs and centipedes, are sometimes introduced into the terrarium via woods moss and logs, because woods moss tends to be a repository for their eggs. Although a daddy-longlegs or a cricket might be fun to observe in a terrarium, it would quickly eat its way through the plants or else starve to death. Furthermore, if crickets escaped from the terrarium, they would eat their way through your clothes and books. Get rid of them just as you would if you found them on your kitchen counter. In a terrarium, pick them out, use an aerosol spray, or water with a Malathion solution.

Earthworms can be really devastating in a terrarium, because they burrow over and over in the same small patch of soil, disturbing and damaging roots as they go. These must be picked out by hand (or with tweezers if you're squeamish) or speared with a fork.

Diseases such as mildews, molds and funguses are easily

detected by the presence of wet rot, soft brown or black leaf spots, blisterlike spots with yellow margins on leaves, leaf distortion, a mildewed, talcum-powdered look on leaves, and masses of grayish threads that resemble bread mold. Besides all that, they make everything in the terrarium look and smell moldy. Most molds feed on dead organic matter, not on living plants. They are unsightly, they block light, and they sometimes spread all over the terrarium. If you see molds or funguses, remove infected plants or leaves, dust the rest with fungicide, and reduce humidity by ventilating—but gradually—for you don't want to subject healthy plants to shock.

Lichens, which looked so pretty when you collected a few pieces in a Baggie last summer, may become a terrarium nuisance, because the humid environment is so beneficial they grow rampantly. You either have to remove them or resign yourself to having a lichen terrarium—which, after all, you might even like.

grooming

Dead or decaying vegetation should be removed as soon as you notice it. Although rotting vegetation gives off carbon dioxide and enriches soil, it is unattractive, sometimes smelly; it promotes growth of funguses and molds; and it takes up space that might be more profitably occupied by healthy, living plants.

On the other hand, your problem may be one of live material—too much of it. If your palms, ferns, or bulbous plants outgrow the terrarium, you will have to remove them or replace them. However, if bushy or vining plants are growing too rampantly, cut back excessive growth. They will become bushier and shapelier and will not outgrow the terrarium as quickly or crowd it up to the point where you can't tell where one plant begins and the next one ends. Do not worry about overcutting. Plants will recuperate quickly from pruning shock because the atmosphere in a terrarium is so good for them.

Maintenance

Names of Plants

COMMON NAME	BOTANICAL NAME
African boxwood	*Myrsine africana*
African violet	*Saintpaulia* sp.
Aluminum plant	*Pilea cadierei*
Arrow-leaf	*Syngonium podophyllum*
Artillery plant	*Pilea microphylla*
Baby's tears	*Helxine soleiroli*
Begonia	*Begonia*
Birdsnest sansevieria	*Sansevieria trifasciata 'Hahnii'*
Bloodleaf	*Iresine herbstii*
Buddhist pine	*Podocarpus macrophylla*
Bugle weed	*Ajuga reptans*
Button fern	*Pellaea rotundifolia*
Caladium, miniature	*Caladium humboldtii*
Checkerberry	*Gaultheria procumbens*
Chinese evergreen	*Aglaomena* sp.
Club moss, dwarf	*Selaginella kraussiana brownii*
Club moss, spreading	*Selaginella kraussiana*
Cobra plant	*Darlingtonia californica*
Copper syngonium	*Syngonium erythrophyllum*
Coral-bead plant	*Nertera depressa*
Coral berry	*Ardisia crispa*
Creeping fig, dwarf	*Ficus pumila minima*
Crystal anthurium	*Anthurium crystallinum*
Earthstar	*Cryptanthus* sp.
Eyelash begonia, miniature	*Begonia bowerii*
Fairy rose	*Rosa chinensis minima*
False African violet	*Streptocarpus saxorum*

Names of Plants

COMMON NAME	BOTANICAL NAME
False heather	*Cuphea hyssopifolia*
False holly, variegated	*Osmanthus ilicifolius*
Fernleaf begonia	*Begonia foliosa*
Firefern	*Oxalis hedysaroides rubra*
Fittonia	*Fittonia verschaffelti*
Flame violet	*Episcia cupreata*
Flamingo flower	*Anthurium scherzerianum*
Floating fern	*Salvinia auriculata rubra*
Floating moss	*Azolla caroliniana*
Golden pothos	*Scindapsus aureus*
Gold-dust dracaena	*Dracaena godseffiana*
Heartleaf philodendron	*Philodendron oxycardium*
Hunters horn	*Sarracenia flava*
Ivy	*Hedera helix* sp.
Jack-in-the-pulpit	*Arisaema triphyllum*
Japanese boxwood	*Buxus microphylla japonica*
Japanese pittosporum	*Pittosporum tobira*
Japanese spindle tree	*Euonymus japonicus*
Kenilworth ivy	*Cymbalaria muralis*
Lace-flower vine	*Episcia dianthiflora*
Lawn leaf	*Dichondra repens*
Lily turf	*Ophiopogon* sp.
Liverwort	*Marchantia polymorpha*
Maidenhair fern, miniature	*Adiantum bellum*
Maranta, miniature	*Calathea micans*
Mexican foxglove	*Allophyton mexicanum*
Mistletoe fig	*Ficus diversifolia*
Myrtle, dwarf	*Myrtus communis microphylla*
Neanthe bella palm	*Chamaedorea elegans 'Bella'*
Parrot's feather	*Myriophyllum proserpinacoides*
Partridgeberry	*Mitchella repens*
Peacock plant	*Calathea makoyana*
Peperomia	*Peperomia obtusifolia*
Peperomia, creeping	*Peperomia prostrata*
Peperomia, miniature	*Pilea depressa*
Pitcher plant	*Nepenthes* sp.
Pothos	*Scindapus aureus*
Prayer plant	*Maranta leuconeura kerchoviana*
Rabbit's foot	*Maranta leuconeura massangeana*
Rainbow fern	*Selaginella uncinata*
Rattlesnake plantain	*Goodyera pubescens*
Resurrection fern	*Polypodium polypodioides*
Ribbon plant	*Dracaena sanderiana*
Ripple peperomia	*Peperomia caperata*
Rosemary	*Rosmarinus officinialis*

The Terrarium Book

COMMON NAME	BOTANICAL NAME
St. Augustine grass, variegated	*Stenotaphrum secundatum variegatum*
Satin pellionia	*Pellionia pulchra*
Sensitive plant	*Mimosa pudica*
Shamrock	*Trifolium repens minus*
Silver-leaf philodendron	*Philodendron sodiroi*
Silver peperomia	*Peperomia metallica*
Silver squill	*Scilla violacea*
Slipper plant, miniature	*Selaginella pusilla*
Sour clover	*Oxalis martiana 'Aureo-reticulatum'*
Spathe flower	*Spathiphyllum 'Clevelandii'*
Spider plant, dwarf	*Chlorophytum bichetii*
Strap fern, dwarf	*Polypodium lycopodioides*
Strawberry begonia	*Saxifraga sarmentosa*
String of hearts	*Ceropegia woodii*
Sundew	*Drosera rotundifolia*
Sweat plant	*Selaginella emmeliana*
Sweet olive	*Osmanthus fragrans*
Sweet pitcher plant	*Sarracenia purpurea*
Table ferns	*Pteris cretica*
Threadleaf sundew	*Drosera filiformis*
Trailing watermelon begonia	*Pellionia daveauana*
Velour philodendron	*Philodendron andreanum*
Velvet-leaf philodendron	*Philodendron verrucosum*
Velvet-leaf vine	*Philodendron micans*
Venus-flytrap	*Dionaea muscipula*
Victoria fern	*Pteris ensiformis 'Victoriae'*
Walking fern	*Adiantum caudatum*
Wandering Jew	*Tradescantia albiflora*
Wandering Jew	*Tradescantia flumensis 'Variegata'*
Wandering Jew	*Zebrina pendula*
Wandering Jew, upright	*Dichorisandra reginae*
Water clover	*Marsilea sp.*
Watercress	*Nasturtium officinale*
Water grass	*Acorus gramineus variegatus*
Water lettuce	*Pistia stratiotes*
Watermelon peperomia	*Peperomia sandersii*
Water pennywort	*Hydrocotyle rotundifolia*
Water poppy	*Hydrocleys commersonii*
Wintergreen	*Gaultheria procumbens*
Yellow-rim serissa	*Serissa foetida variegata*
Zebra plant	*Aphelandra squarrosa 'Louisae'*

Names of Plants

Plant Descriptions

ACORUS GRAMINEUS VARIEGATUS
> FAMILY: Araceae
> ORIGIN: Japan
> TEMPERATURE: Warm
> LIGHT: Medium
> SOIL: Tropical or bog

This water-tolerant dwarf perennial has light-green-and-white variegated irislike leaves that grow in a fan-shaped effect.

ADIANTUM sp.
> FAMILY: Polypodiaceae (Filices)
> TEMPERATURE: Warm
> LIGHT: Medium to low
> SOIL: Tropical

A. bellum is the maidenhair fern from Bermuda with small, light-green, delicate fronds on wiry black stems.

A. caudatum, the "walking fern" from Africa and the Far East, is a small, tufted plant with long, grayish-green, hairy fronds that reach out to root at their tips when they touch the ground, giving the impression of traveling along the soil surface.

AGLAONEMA sp.
> FAMILY: Araceae
> ORIGIN: South Pacific
> TEMPERATURE: Warm
> LIGHT: Medium to low
> SOIL: Tropical

This is the genus that includes the familiar Chinese evergreen. Leaves tend to be lance-shaped and erect. Color is usually dark green, sometimes variegated. Small varieties and young specimens of larger varieties make good terrarium subjects, because they are all slow-growing.

AJUGA REPTANS (Bugle weed)
> FAMILY: Labiatae
> ORIGIN: Orient
> TEMPERATURE: Intermediate
> LIGHT: Medium
> SOIL: Tropical

This member of the mint family forms a flat mass of green leaves that spread easily. Blue, white, red and purplish flowers of the several varieties are held high above leaves. It is often seen in rock gardens and perennial borders but also makes a successful house plant and a very good ground cover for terrariums.

ALLOPHYTON MEXICANUM (Mexican foxglove)
> FAMILY: Scrophulariaceae
> ORIGIN: Mexico, Veracruz

Plant Descriptions

TEMPERATURE: Intermediate
LIGHT: Medium
SOIL: Tropical

This short-stemmed plant has dark-green leathery leaves topped by clusters of trumpet-shaped violet-and-white flowers. Related to the Digitalis (the common foxglove of old-fashioned perennial borders), it is easily grown from seed and is a nearly year-round bloomer.

ANTHURIUM
FAMILY: Araceae
ORIGIN: South America
TEMPERATURE: Warm
LIGHT: Medium to high
SOIL: Tropical or bog

This genus, related to the common philodendron, has some varieties grown primarily for good foliage and others for flowers, but none are favored by both. There are two species small enough for terrariums.

A. crystallinum is grown for its foliage, which has velvety green heart-shaped leaves and contrasting silver-white veins. It is a slow grower.

A. scherzerianum is a native of Costa Rica commonly called flamingo flower, because it is a frequent bloomer sending up fiery red flowers that last several months.

APHELANDRA SQUARROSA
'LOUISAE' (Zebra plant)
FAMILY: Acanthaceae
ORIGIN: Brazil
TEMPERATURE: Warm
LIGHT: Medium to high
SOIL: Tropical

This plant has shiny, emerald-green, rippled leaves brilliantly striped in white. It grows upright and frequently sends up bright-yellow waxy flower heads. Look for the smallest, most compactly growing varieties.

ARDISIA CRISPA (Coral berry)
FAMILY: Myrsinaceae
ORIGIN: China
TEMPERATURE: Intermediate

LIGHT: Medium
SOIL: Tropical

This is actually a large shrub, but seedling plants, which are readily available, grow very slowly and would fit in a moderate-size terrarium for a long time. Leaves are very dark green, elliptically shaped and crinkled at the edges. If the plant is in good light, white flowers will appear in late summer followed by red berries in winter.

ARISAEMA TRIPHYLLUM
(Jack-in-the-pulpit)
FAMILY: Araceae
ORIGIN: Eastern North America
TEMPERATURE: Intermediate
LIGHT: Medium
SOIL: Woodland or tropical

This is a tuberous woodland herb with tall leaves in the middle of which rises a purple-striped green spathe, "the pulpit." A good complement to a woodland or a fern terrarium, it will also add to the curiousness of the bog and carnivorous-plant terrarium.

AZOLLA CAROLINIANA
(Floating moss)
FAMILY: Filices: Salviniaceae
ORIGIN: United States to Argentina
TEMPERATURE: Intermediate
LIGHT: High
SOIL: Bog

Pale-green and reddish leaves form a dense mat making this fern a good ground cover.

BEGONIA
FAMILY: Begoniaceae
TEMPERATURE: Warm
LIGHT: Medium
SOIL: Tropical

There are many miniature begonias that will add color to the terrarium year-round, as most are grown for their multi-hued foliage. Terrariums with begonias should be regularly ventilated and protected from full sun. Some that are freely branching can be trained into bonsai-like shapes.

B. *'Black Falcon'* has black star-shaped taffeta-like leaves, veined in silver-gray, with red undersides and hairy petioles.

B. *boweri*, the miniature eyelash begonia, from Chiapas and Oaxaca, Mexico, has vivid green leaves with blackish patches along the edges.

B. *foliosa*, from Colombia, is called fernleaf begonia, because its trailing stems hold tiny, waxy green fernlike leaves notched at their tips. Flowers are blue-white.

BUXUS MICROPHYLLA JAPONICA (Japanese boxwood)
FAMILY: Buxaceae
ORIGIN: Japan
TEMPERATURE: Intermediate
LIGHT: Medium
SOIL: Tropical

This shrubby evergreen has twiggy stems and small dark-green leathery leaves. Its freely branching habit makes it a good subject for training into topiary, hedge or tree forms.

CALADIUM HUMBOLDTII
FAMILY: Araceae
ORIGIN: Brazil
TEMPERATURE: Warm
LIGHT: Medium
SOIL: Tropical

This variety, one of the smallest of the caladiums, has light-green leaves marked with translucent white spots. It will require winter dormancy; bulbs should be lifted and stored in a cool place for a month or two.

CALATHEA
FAMILY: Marantaceae
ORIGIN: South America
TEMPERATURE: Warm
LIGHT: Medium
SOIL: Tropical

These colorful foliage plants, often mistaken for Marantas, are excellent terrarium subjects because they actually grow most successfully in greenhouse conditions. Two are given here, but many other varieties will do equally well.

C. *makoyana*, from Brazil, is called peacock plant. Leaves are translucent light-green, blotched and lined above with olive-green and below with red.

C. *micans*, from Peru, is one of the smaller of the Calatheas. Its narrow pointed leaves are medium green with silver feathering in the center.

CEROPEGIA WOODII (String of hearts)
FAMILY: Asclepiadaceae
ORIGIN: Natal
TEMPERATURE: Intermediate
LIGHT: Medium to high
SOIL: Tropical

Small heart-shaped fleshy leaves that grow in pairs on long wiry stems are bronze with purple spots if grown in high light, and green with lavender spotting if grown in lower light. Although usually considered a plant for a dry environment, the Ceropegia will grow into a dense mat in a terrarium. Soil should be porous, but the humidity of the terrarium will produce an especially sturdy plant which can be rooted from cuttings or tubers that form at leaf nodes.

CHAMAEDOREA ELEGANS 'BELLA' (Dwarf palm)
FAMILY: Palmae
ORIGIN: Guatemala
TEMPERATURE: Warm
LIGHT: Medium to low
SOIL: Tropical

This small miniature palm with fernlike leaves will withstand low lighting. As the only palm small enough for terrariums, it is one of the most widely used terrarium plants. Seedlings of other palms are sometimes planted in terrariums, but most will outgrow the terrarium too quickly.

CHLOROPHYTUM BICHETII (Dwarf spider plant)
FAMILY: Liliaceae
ORIGIN: Tropical West Africa
TEMPERATURE: Intermediate

LIGHT: Medium
SOIL: Tropical

The variegated grasslike leaves of this small spider plant form clumps like those of its larger relative, but the dwarf form is much smaller, making it an appropriate terrarium subject. Unlike its larger familiar relatives, it does not yield flower stalks and plantlets.

CRYPTANTHUS
FAMILY: Bromeliaceae
ORIGIN: Tropical South America
TEMPERATURE: Warm
LIGHT: Medium
SOIL: Tropical

Cryptanthus are small bromeliads with flattened rosettes of prickly-margined leaves, flecked, speckled, striped, and banded in colors ranging from maroon to lime-green.

CUPHEA HYSSOPIFOLIA
FAMILY: Lythraceae
ORIGIN: Central America
TEMPERATURE: Intermediate
LIGHT: High to medium
SOIL: Tropical

This tiny-leaved, woody shrub has lavender flowers. It is free-branching and can be trained and pruned into treelike forms.

CYMBALARIA MURALIS
(Kenilworth ivy)
FAMILY: Scrophulariaceae
ORIGIN: North Africa
TEMPERATURE: Cool
LIGHT: High
SOIL: Tropical

This creeping perennial ground-cover plant grows easily from seed but needs the high humidity of a terrarium. Clear green leaves are small and kidney-shaped on wiry stems; occasionally small snapdragon-like lilac flowers appear.

DARLINGTONIA CALIFORNICA
(Cobra plant)
FAMILY: Sarraceniaceae
ORIGIN: California and Oregon

TEMPERATURE: Cool
LIGHT: Medium
SOIL: Bog

This plant's yellowish-green leaves tinged with purple grow into erect cobra-headed hoods that have translucent windows whose openings are hidden by purple-spotted forked tongues. Hairs inside the hoods trap flies and fly-sized insects, mealworms or small bits of lean hamburger.

DICHONDRA REPENS (Lawn leaf)
FAMILY: Convolvulaceae
ORIGIN: West Indies
TEMPERATURE: Intermediate
LIGHT: High
SOIL: Tropical

The small, silky round or kidney-shaped leaves of this plant are clear green above and white and hairy below in the juvenile state. Used as ground cover in warm places, it will creep in a terrarium and occasionally send up greenish-yellow flowers.

DICHORISANDRA REGINAE
(Upright Wandering Jew)
FAMILY: Commelinaceae
ORIGIN: Peru
TEMPERATURE: Warm
LIGHT: Medium
SOIL: Tropical

The waxy, dark-green leaves of this plant are silver-spotted and have red centers and purple undersides. Although the plant grows upright, it bears a close resemblance to the more familiar Wandering Jew plant.

DIONAEA MUSCIPULA
(Venus-flytrap)
FAMILY: Droseraceae
ORIGIN: Carolinas
TEMPERATURE: Cool
LIGHT: High to medium
SOIL: Bog

This is the popular meat-eater that everyone likes to feed at cocktail parties. Pale-green leaves grow in rosette fashion; their upper halves form hinged, long-toothed jaws. Trigger hairs inside the jaws attract flies, mealworms or small bits of lean hamburger, which are then caught in the reddish digestive glands within the jaws. Traps will open when food is digested. Do not refeed immediately; let plant rest awhile. High light brings out the reddish coloring.

DRACAENA
FAMILY: Liliaceae
ORIGIN: Africa
TEMPERATURE: Warm
LIGHT: Medium to low
SOIL: Tropical

Any variety of this genus can spend some time in a terrarium, as they are slow growers. They are normally grown in soil on the dry side, but they will adapt to a terrarium especially when the plants are small and young. However, it is important that the soil be especially porous and well drained. The Dracaenas are good subjects for a well-ventilated terrarium.

D. godseffiana, from the Congo, is a durable plant whose leaves are dark green spotted with cream and set in whorls of three on wiry stems. Some improved varieties are spottier and whiter.

D. sanderiana, also from the Congo, has dark-green, lance-shaped leaves bordered in creamy white.

DROSERA (Sundews)
FAMILY: Droseraceae
TEMPERATURE: Cool
LIGHT: High to medium
SOIL: Bog

These small perennial herbs received their common name from the glistening sticky hairs that cover their thread-like and spoon-shaped leaves. If gnats, fruit flies or microscopic pieces of lean meat contact leaves and stems, they stick to sensitive hairs and are digested by sticky fluid from glandular hairs.

D. filiformis, from Atlantic North America, looks like a mass of green threads with red sticky hairs that entrap and digest mosquitoes and small insects.

D. rotundifolia, from North America, is a small rosette of skinny petioles that end in round green pads covered with red hairs that entrap gnats, fruit flies and other small insects.

EPISCIA (Flame violet)
FAMILY: Gesneriaceae
ORIGIN: North and Central America
TEMPERATURE: Warm
LIGHT: Medium
SOIL: Tropical

These are low-growing plants, related to the African violet, with fuzzy oval leaves that form rosettes above which small bell-shaped scarlet, pink, yellow, white and purple flowers are carried. Foliage is usually coppery-green with overtones of metallic pink or silver. They send out runners with plantlets that root easily wherever they touch the soil.

E. cupreata sp. has several varieties that are robust growers with textured leaves in colors ranging from dark mahogany to emerald-green to silver-gray.

E. dianthiflora is a dwarf clustering-rosette plant with dark-green leaves and white flowers.

EUONYMUS
FAMILY: Celastraceae
TEMPERATURE: Cool
LIGHT: Medium to low
SOIL: Tropical

This genus includes shrubs and vines grown indoors, outdoors and in greenhouses. Small-leaved varieties are good terrarium subjects.

E. fortunei uncinatus, from China, is a vining plant with small serrated gray-green leaves with silver-gray midrib and main veins. Its coloring evokes a woodland image.

E. japonicus medio-pictus, from Japan, has an erect stem and 1–1½-inch oval leaves. Many varieties are found in plant and five-and-ten stores, where they are shipped in huge lots from Florida growers. Variegation in leaves

Plant Descriptions

93

ranges from yellow to cream to white. A miniature-leaved form is available.

FICUS (Fig)
FAMILY: Moraceae
TEMPERATURE: Warm
LIGHT: Medium
SOIL: Tropical

This is the genus that includes the common eating fig. We are more familiar with Ficus as large trees including the rubber tree and the banyan tree, but there are two small species suitable for terrariums.

F. diversifolia, from Malaya, is called mistletoe fig, because the olive-green color of the sometimes rounded, sometimes pointed leaves resembles mistletoe and it also bears small yellow fruits. The texture of the leaves is leathery and the tops of the leaves are flecked with tiny white spots not to be confused with insects. It is a slow grower and can be checked by frequent pruning.

F. pumila minima, dwarf creeping fig, is a very slow-growing creeping vine from China with tiny, dark-green quilted leaves. The wiry stems can be trained to grow up the sides of glass or on supports.

FITTONIA VERSCHAFFEL TII
(Fittonia)
FAMILY: Acanthaceae
ORIGIN: Brazil
TEMPERATURE: Warm
LIGHT: Medium
SOIL: Tropical

These are dwarf shrubby vines of prostrate habit whose light-green oval leaves are heavily veined in white, pink or red. They are colorful terrarium subjects and grow well in high humidity.

GAULTHERIA PROCUMBENS
(Checkerberry, Wintergreen)
FAMILY: Ericaceae
ORIGIN: West Coast
TEMPERATURE: Cool
LIGHT: Medium to low
SOIL: Woodland or tropical

Well known to New England woods-watchers, the lustrous green leaves of this plant are used for making tisanes, and its white spring flowers produce edible red berries in fall.

GOODYERA PUBESCENS
(Rattlesnake plantain)
FAMILY: Orchidaceae
ORIGIN: East North America
TEMPERATURE: Cool
LIGHT: Medium to low
SOIL: Woodland

This dwarf orchid is an American native easily collected in East Coast woods areas and widely used in native plant terrariums. Leaves are velvety dark green marked with silver-white veins. Greenish-white flowers are carried on hairy stems.

HEDERA HELIX (Ivy)
FAMILY: Araliaceae
ORIGIN: Global
TEMPERATURE: Cool
LIGHT: Medium
SOIL: Tropical

This is an enormous genus of woody vines whose dark-green leaves are found in many sizes and many shapes. They are easily propagated from cuttings in water or soil and will root from joints if stems are pinned down on soil base. They can be trained (with Scotch tape) to grow up the sides of the terrarium or can be confined to shrubby form by regular pruning. Some of the smaller-leaved varieties good for terrariums are:
H. helix 'Manda's Star'
H. helix 'Shamrock'
H. helix 'Sagittaefolia'
H. helix 'Needlepoint'
H. helix 'Goldheart'
H. helix 'Glacier'

HELXINE SOLEIROLII
(Baby's tears)
FAMILY: Urticaceae
ORIGIN: Corsica, Sardinia
TEMPERATURE: Intermediate
LIGHT: Medium
SOIL: Tropical

The Terrarium Book

This is a tiny-leaved, prostrate herb that makes a good ground cover. High humidity makes it spread rapidly and climb up terrarium walls. If the terrarium has bare spots, little pieces of Helxine pressed into the soil will quickly spread and cover the spot.

HYDROCLEYS COMMERSONII
(Water poppy)
> FAMILY: Butomaceae
> ORIGIN: Brazil, Venezuela
> TEMPERATURE: Warm
> LIGHT: Medium
> SOIL: Bog

This is an aquatic herb for bog terrariums with leathery, oval leaves on long stalks and single yellow flowers.

HYDROCOTYLE ROTUNDIFOLIA
(Water-pennywort)
> FAMILY: Umbelliferae
> ORIGIN: Tropical Asia
> TEMPERATURE: Intermediate
> LIGHT: Medium
> SOIL: Bog

This is a creeping herb with thin rooting stems, cup-shaped, shiny leaves and small white flowers. It will make a good ground cover to complement tall carnivorous plants.

IRESINE HERBSTII (Bloodleaf)
> FAMILY: Amaranthaceae
> ORIGIN: South Brazil
> TEMPERATURE: Intermediate
> LIGHT: High
> SOIL: Tropical

This easily grown small-leaved plant has purplish-red leaves if grown in high light or green if grown in lower light.

MARANTA LEUCONEURA
> FAMILY: Marantaceae
> ORIGIN: Brazil
> TEMPERATURE: Warm
> LIGHT: Medium
> SOIL: Tropical

These low-growing plants belong to the same genus that includes arrowroot and tapioca. The arrowroot received its name when South American Indians discovered it to be a good antidote to arrow wounds.

M. leuconeura kerchoveana is the familiar prayer plant whose chocolate-spotted grayish-green leaves fold up at night, resembling hands folded in prayer.

M. leuconeura massangeana has satiny blue-green leaves with silver-green midribs and thin red lines extending to leaf margins.

MARCHANTIA POLYMORPHA
(Liverwort)
> FAMILY: Marchantiaceae
> ORIGIN: Eastern United States
> TEMPERATURE: Cool
> LIGHT: Medium to low
> SOIL: Bog

This is a primitive-looking low-growing plant that falls botanically somewhere between the mosses and the algae. Green, scale-like leaves have ruffled edges and form dense ground-hugging mats.

MARSILEA sp. (Water clover)
> FAMILY: Filices: Marsileaceae
> ORIGIN: Europe, Africa, Australia
> TEMPERATURE: Warm
> LIGHT: Medium
> SOIL: Bog

These are compact, low-growing ferns whose hairy leaves are shaped like four-leaf clovers and are held delicately on slender stems.

MIMOSA PUDICA (Sensitive plant)
> FAMILY: Leguminosae
> ORIGIN: Brazil
> TEMPERATURE: Warm
> LIGHT: Medium
> SOIL: Tropical or woodland

This short-lived perennial has lacy, light-green leaves that fold up at the slightest touch. If you touch it too frequently, it will go into nervous collapse. The plant is also found in the West Indies, where it is known as the Mori-Vivi (Death-Life) plant.

MITCHELLA REPENS
(Partridgeberry)
>FAMILY: Rubiaceae
>ORIGIN: Eastern North America
>TEMPERATURE: Cool
>LIGHT: Medium
>SOIL: Tropical or woodland

This is the low evergreen creeper with tiny, oval, dark-green leaves and red berries often seen in florists' terrariums at Christmas and commonly found in the New England woods.

MYRIOPHYLLUM
PROSERPINACOIDES (Parrot's feather)
>FAMILY: Haloragidaceae
>ORIGIN: Chile, Uruguay
>TEMPERATURE: Intermediate
>LIGHT: Medium
>SOIL: Bog or tropical

This aquatic herb helps to oxygenate water in ponds. Good for bog terrariums, it has feathery leaves on shoots that rise from a rhizome-like stem that lies submerged in soil.

MYRSINE
>FAMILY: Myrsinaceae
>ORIGIN: Africa and Middle East
>TEMPERATURE: Intermediate
>LIGHT: Medium
>SOIL: Tropical

M. Africana, known as African boxwood, is a shrubby bush, resembling the familiar hedge boxwood, that has thin reddish twiggy stems and small round shiny dark-green leaves. It may be trained into tree form or pruned to shrub form.

M. nummularia, from New Zealand, has tiny glossy round leaves on wiry stems that tend to grow in cascading tiers.

MYRTUS COMMUNIS
MICROPHYLLA (Dwarf myrtle)
>FAMILY: Myrtaceae
>ORIGIN: Mediterranean
>TEMPERATURE: Intermediate
>LIGHT: Medium
>SOIL: Tropical

A tiny-leaved, dark-green shrub, this dwarf form of the classic Greek myrtle can be trained to grow in tree form or allowed to develop as a shrub. Prune frequently. Cuttings root readily.

NASTURTIUM OFFICINALE
(Watercress)
>FAMILY: Cruciferae
>ORIGIN: Europe
>TEMPERATURE: Cool
>LIGHT: Medium
>SOIL: Bog or tropical

This is the familiar salad herb that grows in marshes and along shorelines, making it a good subject for a bog terrarium. Tiny white flowers appear sometimes over clumps of dark-green leaves.

NEPENTHES sp. (Pitcher plant)
>FAMILY: Nepenthaceae
>ORIGIN: Tropical Asia
>TEMPERATURE: Warm
>LIGHT: Medium
>SOIL: Bog

These inhabitants of the Asian monsoon areas have leathery leaves and broadened petioles that develop into pendulous hollow pitchers with thick rims and lids that keep rain out. Insects and mealworms are trapped inside by honey glands and drown in digestive juices. They should be grown in soil mix No. 1 for bog and carnivorous plants.

NERTERA DEPRESSA
(Coral-bead plant)
>FAMILY: Rubiaceae
>ORIGIN: Peru, Cape Horn, New Zealand
>TEMPERATURE: Cool
>LIGHT: Medium
>SOIL: Bog or tropical

An exquisite low-growing mat of tiny round leaves and bright persimmon-colored berries, this charmer will set its berries if kept very cool in summer and always moist. In the Andes and in New Zealand it grows on water-covered rocks.

OPHIOPOGON sp. (Lily-turf)
    FAMILY: Lilaceae
    ORIGIN: China, Japan
    TEMPERATURE: Cool to intermediate
    LIGHT: Medium
    SOIL: Tropical

This genus includes a variety of grass-like clustering, narrow-leaved plants. Foliage is usually dark green, occasionally banded in white. The Ophiopogons are closely related to and sometimes confused with Liriope.

OSMANTHUS
    FAMILY: Oleaceae
    ORIGIN: China
    TEMPERATURE: Cool to intermediate
    LIGHT: Medium to high
    SOIL: Tropical

These are evergreen shrubs from the same family as the Roman olive tree. They grow slowly, produce fragrant white flowers, and can be pruned to be kept within bounds.

O. fragrans, sweet olive, has leathery, dark-green, serrated leaves and tiny white flowers. The Chinese use the foliage to flavor tea. High light produces flowers that can scent an entire room.

O. ilicifolius variegatus, false holly, is a slow-growing shrub with green and white variegated hollylike serrated leaves.

OXALIS
    FAMILY: Oxalidaceae
    TEMPERATURE: Intermediate
    LIGHT: High
    SOIL: Tropical

This is a bulbous group of plants with familiar shamrock leaves from the wood-sorrel family. Some have flowers, if grown in full sun; all need an annual period of dormancy, particularly after blooming. Oxalis should be grown somewhat drier than most terrarium plants. You can either group them with plants that have similar needs or, when you terrace the terrarium landscape, set them on a level above the other plants so you can water them separately. They can be used most effectively in open terrariums.

O. hedysaroides rubra, called firefern, is an erect, shrubby plant from South America with wiry stems and small wine-red leaves consisting of three heart-shaped leaflets. Flowers are lemon-yellow.

O. martiana 'Aureo-reticulata,' the sour-clover from tropical America, has deep-green leaves with three leaflets veined in yellow. Stems grow low and high, and flowers are carmine-red with white throats.

PELLAEA ROTUNDIFOLIA
(Button fern)
    FAMILY: Filices
    ORIGIN: New Zealand
    TEMPERATURE: Warm
    LIGHT: Medium
    SOIL: Tropical

This is a small rock-loving fern with long, thin fronds. The plant stays compact and low-growing; it serves as a good ground cover.

PELLIONIA
    FAMILY: Urticaceae
    ORIGIN: Vietnam
    TEMPERATURE: Warm
    LIGHT: Medium
    SOIL: Tropical

Pellionias are ground creepers with fleshy leaves and pinkish stems.

P. daveauana has thin, fleshy oval leaves as a small plant, has lance-shaped gray-green leaves bordered in dark purplish brown.

P. pulchra has elongated oval gray-green leaves ribbed and veined in reddish brown.

PEPEROMIA
    FAMILY: Piperaceae
    TEMPERATURE: Warm
    LIGHT: Medium
    SOIL: Tropical

Peperomias are clustering or trailing

plants with waxy, oval leaves usually striped or otherwise variegated. They do well in open terrariums, because they should not be kept too wet or they will develop stem rot.

P. caperata from Brazil, the Emerald Ripple peperomia, is a sturdy plant of clustering habit. Its forest-green-and-chocolate leaves are quilted and corrugated and reverse to pale-green.

P. metallica from Peru has narrow coppery leaves banded in silver and veined in red with dark reddish stems.

P. prostrata, from Colombia, is a tiny creeper with minute brown to blue-gray waxy leaves etched in silver on thin reddish vines.

P. sandersii, from Brazil, is known as the watermelon peperomia, because its fleshy, bluish-green leaves are banded with silver stripes emanating from the center vein of the leaf.

PHILODENDRON
FAMILY: Araceae
ORIGIN: Tropical South America
TEMPERATURE: Warm
LIGHT: Medium to low
SOIL: Tropical

The name philodendron comes from the Greek *phileo*, to love, and *dendron*, a tree, referring to the habit of this genus to overrun trees in the South American forests. There are many unusual philodendrons that are worthy of greater cultivation — especially some varieties that love high humidity, thus making them excellent terrarium subjects.

P. andreanum has iridescent velvety dark-olive-green leaves suffused with copper and veined in ivory.

P. micans is a leggy vine with small, heart-shaped, coppery-green velvety leaves with red undersides.

P. sodiroi has predominantly silver-green leaves veined and bordered in dark-green. Only in the juvenile stage can it be grown in the terrarium.

P. variifolium is a slow-growing vine with heart-shaped bluish-green leaves banded in silver.

P. verrucosum has velvety dark-bronzed-green leaves veined in dark green and margined in light green. The undersides of the leaves are coppery; the petioles are dark red covered with greenish hairs. Its rippled shape and unusual coloring make this a dramatic accent plant in the terrarium.

PILEA
FAMILY: Urticaceae
TEMPERATURE: Warm
LIGHT: Medium
SOIL: Tropical

Pileas want a somewhat drier atmosphere than most terrarium plants. Ventilation in the terrarium would help. Hairy-leaved varieties are more subject to rot.

P. cadierei, aluminum plant, from Vietnam, has green, rippled foliage highlighted in silver. The variety 'Minima' is a dwarf form.

P. depressa, from Puerto Rico, is a free-branching, glossy, pea-green succulent creeper. It roots readily at leaf nodes.

P. microphylla, artillery plant, from the West Indies, has light-green stems and leaves and a fernlike look.

PISTIA STRATIOTES (Water lettuce)
FAMILY: Araceae
ORIGIN: Tropical America
TEMPERATURE: Warm
LIGHT: Medium
SOIL: Bog or tropical

Bright-green velvety leaf rosettes and small green flowers hug the soil and spread easily, making this an excellent ground cover for the bog terrarium.

PITTOSPORUM TOBIRA
FAMILY: Pittosporaceae
ORIGIN: China
TEMPERATURE: Intermediate to cold
LIGHT: Medium to low
SOIL: Tropical

The glossy dark-green oval leaves make this plant a good accent for the terrarium. Small plants are slow-growing and can be kept small if they are pruned regularly.

PODOCARPUS MACROPHYLLA
(Buddhist pine)
> FAMILY: Podocarpaceae
> ORIGIN: China, Japan
> TEMPERATURE: Intermediate
> LIGHT: Medium
> SOIL: Tropical

These are needle-leaved, many-branched shrubby plants that tend to be thin and willowy. They need frequent attention to pruning and they root easily from cuttings.

POLYPODIUM
> FAMILY: Filices
> TEMPERATURE: Warm
> LIGHT: Medium
> SOIL: Tropical

P. lycopodioides, the dwarf strap fern from the West Indies, is a dwarfed creeper with leathery, undivided straplike fronds.

P. polypodioides, from the East Coast and tropical America, is called resurrection fern. Its small, leathery fronds curl up and appear to die when dry, then revive when moistened.

PTERIS
> FAMILY: Filices
> ORIGIN: Tropics and subtropics
> TEMPERATURE: Intermediate
> LIGHT: Medium to low
> SOIL: Tropical

P. cretica are a group of small, upright, lacy, light-green ferns, called table ferns. Fronds are serrated and ruffled, sometimes variegated white and silver.

P. ensiformis 'Victoriae,' sometimes referred to as Victoria fern, has short sterile fronds and erect, tall fertile fronds banded white and edged green.

ROSA CHINENSIS MINIMA
(Fairy rose)
> FAMILY: Rosaceae
> ORIGIN: China
> TEMPERATURE: Intermediate
> LIGHT: High
> SOIL: Tropical

Once thought to be lost to horticulture, the fairy rose was rediscovered on a window sill of a cottage in Switzerland where it was originally developed as an indoor pot plant. By itself in a single-plant terrarium, such as a dome, it is beautiful and more easily cared for than in a multiple planting. The tiny double flowers and green foliage that perfectly mimic familiar hybrid teas (including thorns!) need special attention. Terrariums with roses need frequent ventilation; if humidity is too high, it will provoke the fungus and bacterial diseases all roses are prey to. Soil should be constantly moist, but never soggy, and light must be excellent for flowering. Several varieties are available in white, red, pink and yellow.

ROSMARINUS OFFICINIALIS
(Rosemary)
> FAMILY: Labiatae
> ORIGIN: Mediterranean
> TEMPERATURE: Intermediate
> LIGHT: High
> SOIL: Tropical

This needle-leaved, aromatic, shrubby plant can be pruned to tree shape. Clippings are used as seasoning, and it roots easily from cuttings.

SAINTPAULIA sp. (African violets)
> FAMILY: Gesneriaceae
> ORIGIN: Africa
> TEMPERATURE: Warm
> LIGHT: Medium
> SOIL: Tropical

As the most discussed and widely grown indoor plant in the United States, the African violet is the French poodle of indoor gardeners. Nearly everyone loves to grow them, and no one agrees on how to do it. The genus includes many original varieties and as many hybrid varieties of these fuzzy-leaved, rosette-like plants, but the dwarf varieties are best suited for

Plant Descriptions

terrariums. These need good light, a porous, humusy soil and plenty of air circulation. Use them in well-ventilated terrariums, and watch for fungus diseases. Pick off dead leaves promptly. When misting, avoid wetting the foliage.

SALVINIA AURICULATA
(Floating fern)
> FAMILY: Filices: Salviniaceae
> ORIGIN: Tropical America
> TEMPERATURE: Warm
> LIGHT: High
> SOIL: Bog or tropical

This small aquatic fern has pale-yellow-green leaves set on floating rhizomes that will rest on soil and colonize in the terrarium. The plant is especially suited to bog terrariums.

SANSEVIERIA TRIFASCIATA
'HAHNII' (Birdsnest sansevieria)
> FAMILY: Liliaceae
> ORIGIN: New Orleans
> TEMPERATURE: Intermediate
> LIGHT: Low to medium
> SOIL: Tropical

Most sansevierias (familiarly known as snake plants) are much too large for terrariums, but this one is a low-growing rosette of dark-green leaves with paler green crossbanding. It suckers freely and gives a vase-like effect.

SARRACENIA (Hunter's horn)
> FAMILY: Sarraceniaceae
> ORIGIN: Eastern seaboard
> TEMPERATURE: Cool
> LIGHT: High to medium
> SOIL: Bog

These herbaceous perennials have hollow fluted leaves, winged on one side and lidded, which hold liquid the way a pitcher does. Sugary juices emanating from the mouth of the plants attract flies, beetles and spiders, which cannot escape because inside hairs trap them and they are digested and absorbed into the bottom of the pitchers. Soil mix No. 1 for carnivorous plants is recommended. Feeding is not necessary; if you like, you can give plants mealworms and hamburger.

S. flava, called yellow pitcher plant, has tall, slender tubes that are light-green or crimson.

S. purpurea, called the Northern pitcher plant as it is found in Maryland, has low-growing green and rusty red rosettes veined in crimson with hairy throats and lids. Purple flowers are carried high on tall slender stalks.

SAXIFRAGA SARMENTOSA
(Strawberry begonia)
> FAMILY: Saxifragaceae
> ORIGIN: China, Japan
> TEMPERATURE: Intermediate to cool
> LIGHT: Medium to high
> SOIL: Tropical

This low-growing fuzzy-leaved plant, which sends out many runners that have plantlets attached, is neither a strawberry nor a begonia. It does flower, bearing its small white blooms on tall stems well above the foliage. It should be grown slightly on the dry side. Color is bluish green marked with silver; there is also a smaller variety, 'Tricolor,' whose leaves are also tinged with pink.

SCILLA VIOLACEA
> FAMILY: Liliaceae
> ORIGIN: South Africa
> TEMPERATURE: Intermediate
> LIGHT: Medium
> SOIL: Tropical

This small bulbous plant suckers freely. It has variegated lance-shaped silver leaves with green-blotched and dark-red undersides. Small blue and green flowers carried on stalks appear in winter.

SCINDAPSUS
> FAMILY: Araceae
> ORIGIN: South Pacific
> TEMPERATURE: Warm
> LIGHT: Medium to low
> SOIL: Tropical

These are vining plants often confused with Philodendrons, but most of these are variegated.

S. aureus, pothos, is a fleshy-leaved climber with green and yellow variegated leaves. 'Marble Queen' variety is variegated in white.

S. pictus has small waxy leaves blotched in silver that tend to flatten out against the stems.

SELAGINELLA
FAMILY: Selaginellaceae
ORIGIN: Tropical Asia
TEMPERATURE: Intermediate
LIGHT: Medium
SOIL: Tropical or bog

The light, lacy, dark-green leaves of this low grower make it look like a cross between a moss and a fern. It is easily rooted and will grow up the sides of terrarium walls until its own weight pulls it down. It can be pruned to be kept in check, but the roots are delicate, so transplanting should be handled carefully. It spreads easily, and loves high humidity, thus making it one of the best terrarium ground covers.

S. emmeliana is the Sweat plant from South America whose lacy, bright-green leaves grow in rosette fashion producing a ferny effect.

S. kraussiana, Spreading club moss, is a mosslike creeper with scaly leaves. It is a low-growing good ground cover.

S. kraussiana brownii, Dwarf club moss, forms hemispherical clumps or cushions. Its rich green foliage makes it a good subject for the small, single-plant terrarium.

S. uncinata is similar to, but coarser textured than, *S. kraussiana*. It is a low creeper whose coloring is iridescent blue-green.

SERISSA FOETIDA VARIEGATA
FAMILY: Rubiaceae
ORIGIN: Japan, China
TEMPERATURE: Cool
LIGHT: Medium to high

SOIL: Tropical

A small, shrubby plant that never grows more than two feet high, it branches freely and can be pruned to keep it very small. Leaves are tiny, dark-green, and bordered in white. As it does not need extremely high humidity, it is a good subject for a partly open terrarium.

SINNINGIA (Dwarf gloxinia)
FAMILY: Gesneriaceae
ORIGIN: Brazil
TEMPERATURE: Warm
LIGHT: Medium
SOIL: Tropical

These are tiny, dainty little plants that are sometimes called miniature gloxinias, which they are related to and closely resemble. Clusters of puckered small leaves and little bell-shaped flowers are often no larger than one by one inch, making them perfect bloomers for tiny terrariums.

S. concinna has small hairy green leaves with red stalks and veins and purplish and white flowers.

S. pusilla is a tiny rosette of oval puckered leaves colored olive-green with brown veins. Flowers are orchid and lemon.

SPATHIPHYLLUM 'CLEVELANDII'
(Spathe flower)
FAMILY: Araceae
ORIGIN: South America
TEMPERATURE: Warm
LIGHT: Medium to low
SOIL: Tropical

The young spathiphyllums with their tall clustering leaves will grow well in and add a lush, reedy look to the terrarium. If grown in good light, large white flowers appear from time to time.

STENOTAPHRUM SECUNDATUM VARIEGATUM (St. Augustine grass var.)
FAMILY: Gramineae
ORIGIN: Florida, Tropical America

TEMPERATURE: Intermediate
LIGHT: Medium to high
SOIL: Tropical

The common St. Augustine is a major lawn grass in southern Florida. A close relative of the bamboo, it has flattened stems that root easily at the nodes and has dark-green, creamy-white banded leaves that lend a grassy texture to a terrarium planting.

STREPTOCARPUS SAXORUM
FAMILY: Gesneriaceae
ORIGIN: Africa
TEMPERATURE: Warm
LIGHT: Medium
SOIL: Tropical

This is a small spreading plant closely related to the African violet, with fleshy, yellow-green leaves and white and lilac flowers borne on long, slender stalks.

SYNGONIUM
FAMILY: Araceae
ORIGIN: Tropical America
TEMPERATURE: Warm
LIGHT: Medium to low
SOIL: Tropical

These are vining plants whose dark-green leaves are mostly arrow-shaped. They must be pruned frequently and regularly to preserve the juvenile state where the foliage is prettiest and plants small enough for terrariums.

S. erythrophyllum has small arrow-shaped dark-green leaves with a coppery cast flecked in silver pink.

S. podophyllum, the Nephthytis of the florist's trade, has thin, large, arrow-shaped green leaves on slender petioles in the juvenile state and heavily lobed leaves in its mature state. Many varieties are available in varying forms and colors.

TRADESCANTIA
FAMILY: Commelinaceae
ORIGIN: Tropical America

TEMPERATURE: Intermediate
LIGHT: Medium
SOIL: Tropical

This genus includes several attractive multicolored creepers that root easily at leaf nodes, making them good ground covers. If plants grow too rampantly, prune heavily.

T. albiflora includes the variety 'Albo-vittata,' with fleshy lance-shaped bluish-green and white leaves, and the variety 'Laekenensis' that has smaller, more delicate pale-green and white leaves tinted purple. Both can be trained to grow up walls.

T. flumensis 'Variegata' has shiny light-green leaves striped in yellow and cream. Prune often to keep within bounds; cuttings can be rooted anywhere to fill bare spots in the terrarium.

TRIFOLIUM REPENS MINUS
(Irish shamrock)
FAMILY: Leguminosae
ORIGIN: Ireland
TEMPERATURE: Cool
LIGHT: High
SOIL: Tropical

These are the tiny three-leaved clovers everyone buys on St. Patrick's Day. They make excellent creepers and ground covers and in fact will grow much more successfully in a terrarium than in a pot.

ZEBRINA PENDULA (Wandering Jew or Tradescantia)
FAMILY: Commelinaceae
ORIGIN: Mexico
TEMPERATURE: Intermediate
LIGHT: Medium
SOIL: Tropical

The small pointed leaves of this trailer are green and purple banded in silver. A good grower, the plant has long stems which make a good ground cover, can be trained to climb up terrarium walls, or can be pruned to keep in check. See also Tradescantia.

About the Authors

CHARLES M. EVANS is a horticulturist, known particularly as the nation's leading authority on the lighting of plants. He studied horticulture and molecular biology at the University of Florida, worked in Florida's botanical gardens, and has taught and practiced in Miami and Detroit. He is currently living and working in New York City.

ROBERTA LEE PLINER is a free-lance writer originally from New England, where she learned to garden in Rhode Island and on Cape Cod. Miss Pliner and Mr. Evans have co-authored several magazine articles on plants, and although this is their first book collaboration, other volumes are on their way. Miss Pliner lives in New York City.